CHRIST AND THE CC

A Reformulation of Trinitaria

The concept of the 'social Trinity', which posits three conscious subjects in God, radically revised the traditional Christian idea of the Creator. It promoted a view of God as a passionate, creative, and responsive source of all being. Keith Ward argues that social Trinitarian thinking threatens the unity of God, however, and that this new view of God does not require a 'social' component. Expanding on the work of such theologians as Barth and Rahner, who insisted that there was only one mind of God, Ward offers a coherent, wholly monotheistic interpretation of the Trinity. *Christ and the Cosmos* analyses theistic belief in a scientific context, demonstrating the necessity of cosmology to theological thinking that is often overly myopic and anthropomorphic. This important volume will benefit those who seek to understand what the Trinity is, why it matters, and how it fits into a scientific account of the universe.

KEITH WARD is Professorial Research Fellow at Heythrop College, London, and Fellow of the British Academy. He was formerly Regius Professor of Divinity and a Canon of Christ Church at the University of Oxford. His numerous publications include *The Evidence for God: The Case for the Existence of the Spiritual Dimension*; *Morality, Autonomy, and God*; and the five-volume *Comparative Theology*.

CHRIST AND THE COSMOS

A Reformulation of Trinitarian Doctrine

KEITH WARD

Heythrop College, London

CAMBRIDGE
UNIVERSITY PRESS

CAMBRIDGE
UNIVERSITY PRESS

32 Avenue of the Americas, New York NY 10013-2473, USA

Cambridge University Press is part of the University of Cambridge.

It furthers the University's mission by disseminating knowledge in the pursuit of education, learning and research at the highest international levels of excellence.

www.cambridge.org
Information on this title: www.cambridge.org/9781107531819

© Keith Ward 2015

First published 2015

A catalogue record for this publication is available from the British Library

Library of Congress Cataloguing in Publication data
Ward, Keith, 1938–
Christ and the cosmos : a reformulation of trinitarian doctrine / Keith Ward,
Heythrop College, London.
pages cm
Includes bibliographical references and index.
1. Trinity.   I. Title.
BT111.3.W36   2015
231'.044–dc23   2015011156

ISBN 978-1-107-53181-9 Paperback

Contents

PART V THE COSMIC TRINITY

Preface

Many people would be surprised if I said that one of the most important questions in the world today is whether there is a God and what God is like. For such people, God has become irrelevant, and practical problems of world hunger, injustice, and ecological disaster are obviously much more important. Those problems are very important, of course. Yet if there is a God, that may be literally of *eternal* importance. Thinking about God does not in any way prevent trying to tackle practical problems such as that of world hunger – it ought to reinforce efforts to resolve such problems – but it does add another important question to the list of things that are worthy of consideration.

Suppose God is an objective reality of supreme beauty, wisdom, and goodness, and that God has a purpose for the universe, which is, in part, that humans should find their greatest happiness and fulfilment in knowing and cooperating with that supreme goodness. That would make a huge difference to human life. It would give every human life an overriding purpose, meaning, and value, as well as a real hope of achieving a truly worthwhile fulfilment.

I have written this book in the belief that there is such a God. I have written it in a context in which many people have dismissed the idea of God as somehow incoherent or even objectionable. Further, I am a Christian who believes that God is a Trinity, 'three persons in one substance', as the tradition puts it. And this is widely thought to be especially absurd. Three into one won't go! I want to put the case that the idea of the Trinity is a profound and intellectually penetrating idea and that it embodies a spirituality – a way of living in dynamic and life-enhancing relation to transcendent values – that can change human lives for the better.

I am not alone. There has been a lot of discussion about the Trinity among Christian theologians in the past century. Much of it has been concerned with developing a fairly new idea of God as dynamic, relational, responsive, and other-creating. Instead of being thought of as a changeless, rather impersonal and impassive being (like the God of Aristotle or the supreme Good of Plato), God has been reconfigured as a continually changing creator of the universe who responds to it and reacts to it in ever-new ways, who feels its pains, and who cooperates with it to create new forms of value and experience.

Part of this widespread (but not universal!) revision has been the development of what has been called the 'social Trinity'. This is the idea that there is one divine being in which there are three subjects of consciousness and action, inseparably joined in a union of mutual love and self-giving, which then spreads out into the universe. The central argument of this book is that the idea of God as other-creating dynamic love is an illuminating one and is fully consistent with many central strands of Biblical insight. But the idea of God as a sort of society is a bad idea. It is repugnant to Jews, Muslims, and many monotheists (including me), and it has great disadvantages that its proponents have not fully recognised. Among them can often be found a sort of unintended arrogance that presumes to say exactly what God is in the divine being itself, as opposed to saying how God truly appears to finite human minds. So as well as attacking the 'social' view of the Trinity, I also attack the claim, sometimes made, that the phrase 'Father, Son, and Holy Spirit' must be unrevisably and unsurpassably true of the divine being in itself. I think any such claim is inconsistent with the belief, also common in Christian traditions, that God is essentially beyond full human understanding – even though God can reveal the divine nature in ways suitable for human understanding.

Much traditional Christian imagery of the Trinity needs radical revision. When the planet earth was believed to stand at the centre of creation, when the stars were thought to be lamps hanging in the sky, and when humans were thought to be the most advanced beings in the universe, the old iconography, found in thousands of paintings – a bearded human figure, a young man hanging on a cross, and a bird – was understandable. Now that we know there are a hundred billion stars in the Milky Way, a hundred billion galaxies in the observable universe, and possibly untold numbers of universes other than this one, that imagery has become unjustifiably myopic.

What could beings from other galaxies make of it? Would they know anything at all about human primates, crosses, and birds, much less think that such entities were ultimate realities behind this enormous universe? Christian theologians have, of course, usually said that God is infinite and the creator of this and maybe of many universes (St. Augustine, for instance, said that, in *The City of God*, Book 12, chapter 19). They have said that God is beyond not only this space-time, but beyond all space-times. So they have not seriously thought that God looks like a human primate or a bird. These are symbols, appropriate for humans on this small blue planet.

Beyond this planet, they usually thought there were ranks of superior spiritual beings – among them angels, archangels, cherubim, seraphim, and thrones. Humans were not the highest form of personal life. But when represented in art, angelic powers were strangely humanoid too. This led to a certain limitation of imagination, as though God had shrunk to manageable, all-too-human size. In some ways the traditional symbols have become obstacles to, rather than vehicles of, spiritual insight. This seems particularly so when some modern theologians say that God is essentially Father, Son, and Spirit, and can only be described as such. Some of them have said that the 'economic Trinity', the way God appears and acts in relation to humans on this planet, is actually identical with the 'immanent Trinity', the way the creator and sustainer of infinite space really and essentially is.

I think we need to break out of such limiting, and unduly human-centred, thinking. But this is not an attempt to dispense with the Christian doctrine of the Trinity. On the contrary, it is an attempt to re-state in a stronger form and with a truly fundamental, cosmic perspective the importance of that doctrine. In that sense, it is in line with the New Testament itself, which clearly sees Christ as a cosmic figure (in the first chapters of the Letters to the Ephesians and the Colossians, for example). It is in line with third- and fourth-century attempts to see Christianity in truly cosmic terms. It just happened that the cosmos was thought to be really small in those days. It was small in space, so humans were the only material personal beings that existed. It was small in time, so it had begun not long ago – and was due to end at any moment.

Now we know that humans are on the periphery of a vast universe and that the end of this planet or of the whole human race would have minimal effect on most of that universe. So we need to re-image the Trinity in cosmic terms. For Christians, Jesus represents the uniting of finite reality, in the form of a human being, with the infinite spiritual reality of God. In relation to him, and therefore to us, God appears as Father, the one who brings finite persons into being, cares for their ultimate well-being, and works to bring them to mature freedom and fully loving relationships. The union of finite and infinite that was manifest in Jesus is made possible for other generations of humans by the work of the Spirit, which is God present in the innermost being of members of the human species.

It does not matter that we are on the periphery of the universe and that we will probably die out as a species in the blink of a cosmic eye. We in our small corner of the universe will have been united to Eternity through the actions of the God who has been revealed to us in the form of one who was Son of God and Son of Man as well as the Father and Spirit of that Son. That leads to the hope – indeed the expectation – that this same God will act in relevantly similar ways wherever in this vast universe there are sentient and personal beings capable of conscious union with the divine. It leads to the postulate that God will act in alien worlds and among alien forms of life, if there are any, with a similar threefold form, manifesting in other modes of finite personal reality, acting in their innermost lives, and leading them to union with the divine. There will be a Trinity, a threefoldness, even though it seems rather unlikely to take specific form as a father, a son, and a 'breath of life'.

Once we see the relativity of specific symbols for the threefold-ness of the cosmic God, we are in a good position to see the inadequacy of accounts of the Trinity which tie themselves too tightly to particular symbols which are taken to be definitive, absolute, and universal. Some accounts of the 'immanent Trinity' seem to be little more than projections of the 'economic Trinity' directly and without change onto an otherwise unknown 'immanent Trinity'. Our view of the economic Trinity does indeed have implications for our view of what the divine being in itself is – for God must be such that the threefold form in which God relates to creation is a genuine and ineliminable feature of Being itself. In that sense, God really and ultimately is a Trinitarian God. But I argue that projecting the economic Trinity in precisely the form it takes in relation to this planet onto the divine being in itself is the result of an unacknowledged commitment to the philosophical doctrine of naive realism, which holds that reality must be just the way we perceive it to be. That doctrine, I suggest, is rightly regarded by most of those who have considered it as both implausible and misleading.

In a similar way, there is often a commitment to the implausible philosophical doctrine that persons are essentially and wholly constituted by their social relationships and that self-knowledge is only possible if an 'other' is posited in which the self can be objectified and reflected. These doctrines, which are mostly Hegelian or Marxist in origin, are illuminating when applied to social and historically developing animals such as human beings. But it is very difficult to take them as definitive of all possible types of personal realities. The consequent notions of 'personhood' and of what a divine being must necessarily be like are, I argue, unduly dogmatic and restrictive. If such dogmatism can be overcome, I argue that 'social' and 'psychological' interpretations of the Trinity, when closely analysed, are not in polar opposition to one another, but rather reflect complementary emphases which may, and I think should, readily converge.

This is not a historical work, detailing the development of Trinitarian doctrine. There are many very good books which have done this work with admirable scholarship. Instead, I look at some of the best-known theological proposals in recent theology from the beginning of the twentieth century. By critical engagement with them, I build up a doctrine of the Trinity which is meant to be not a rejection but an authentic development of traditional concerns and to constitute a re-working of the doctrine that will have plausibility and practical significance in the scientific age.

This is therefore partly a polemical book, with a case to argue. But my subject is not just a sort of internal Christian quarrel, of little interest to anyone else. It raises deep human questions about the nature of ultimate reality and of how much humans can hope to understand of that reality. It raises perennial philosophical questions about such puzzling concepts as 'substance', 'person', 'cause', 'time', and 'explanation'. And it raises pressing personal questions about what is a good human life, how one can find value and purpose in one's own life, and whether and how one can consciously relate to the ultimately real.

Recent arguments about the Trinity express fundamental perspectives on human being and on the reality within which humans exist. I approach these arguments not only as a theologian, but also as a philosopher trained in the analytical tradition. I stand in a relatively new tradition which may be called 'analytical theology', for which the insistence on clarity, precision, and the formal analysis of language that has marked analytical philosophy is applied to the basic claims of the Christian faith. This often leads to new ways of stating doctrines about God, the Incarnation of God in Jesus, and the Trinity. But this is in no way a rejection of Christian faith as stated in the Nicene Creed or the formulae of the Council of Chalcedon. It is a recognition that early classical Christian formulations of doctrine were influenced by basically Greek philosophical viewpoints that no longer command the assent of most contemporary thinkers, whether Christian or not. If the same faith assertions are to be sustained today, they must be stated in different ways, using concepts and background presuppositions from our post-Enlightenment and post-modern context. I accept that modern philosophical interpretations, which are in any case very diverse, will themselves stand in need of future revision. My aim is simply to provide a contribution, from my own perspective, to contemporary debate about the Trinity and to reflection on the nature of what most religious believers call God – that which is of ultimate value and reality, the nature of which Christians believe to be definitively disclosed in Jesus Christ.

Acknowledgements

I am grateful to my colleagues in the Faculty of Theology at Oxford University for their (often unknowing) help in the development of the ideas in this book, and especially to Dr. Robert Morgan, whose scholarly understanding of the New Testament was invaluable. I would also like to thank the anonymous readers of the book for Cambridge University Press, who made many very helpful suggestions. Thanks are due, also, to Heythrop College, London, for the encouragement they gave me to write the book. Not least, I am always grateful to Marian, my wife, who has unfailingly supported my work throughout many years.

All Biblical quotations are from the New Revised Standard Version.

PART I

The Threefold Nature of the Divine Being

CHAPTER I

Introduction: Talking about the Trinity

'In the name of the Father, the Son, and the Holy Spirit ...' These are familiar words to millions of people throughout the world who accept the Christian faith. Yet they can be troublesome. To many Jews and Muslims, it sounds as if Christians believe in three gods. The Qur'an says, 'They blaspheme who say "God is one of three in a Trinity"' (Qur'an 5, 76). And many Christians would be at a loss if they had to say exactly what the Trinity is, and how God could be, in the words of the technical definition, 'three persons in one substance'. I have even met Christian clergy who dread having to preach about the Trinity on Trinity Sunday, or who make do with some vastly oversimplified version which has little connection with any established theological traditions.

In my own church, the Church of England, on thirteen days of the year the Athanasian Creed is appointed by the Prayer Book to be recited by the congregation at Morning Prayer. That creed says, among other things, 'There is one Person of the Father, another of the Son: and another of the Holy Ghost ... and yet they are not three incomprehensibles, nor three uncreated: but one uncreated, and one incomprehensible.' It is perhaps not surprising that I have never heard this creed publicly recited – except that I once made a congregation do so, and most of the worshippers had to smother a laugh when they came to that part.

It is clearly possible to state the doctrine of the Trinity in ways that make little sense to a modern congregation. Yet belief in God as Trinity is central to Christian faith. Indeed, in the late twentieth century Christian theologians began to put renewed emphasis on the doctrine. The English theologian Leonard Hodgson was one of the first to argue explicitly that God is not just a personal being with one consciousness and will (Hodgson, 1943). The Christian God is, he held, an organic unity of three persons, with differing personal histories. Other theologians – David Brown, Wolfhart Pannenberg, John Zizioulas, Colin Gunton, Robert Jenson, Richard Swinburne, and William Hasker among them – have strongly argued that seeing God as a social entity (I know 'entity' is an inadequate term, but let it pass for now) is more devotionally satisfactory than seeing God as a sort of isolated, lonely mind. The influential German theologian Jurgen Moltmann even wrote that monotheism is a doctrine that leads to autocracy and hierarchy, whereas Trinitarian belief is much more democratic and egalitarian.

The point can be put by contrasting Aristotle's idea of God with that of Wolfhart Pannenberg. For Aristotle, God is a supremely perfect being, unchanging and uncaused, whose supreme beatitude consists in contemplating its own perfection. Pannenberg regards this idea of God as supremely egocentric, the supreme case of self-love – and therefore not perfect at all. Rather, he says, 'God is love – *ho theos agape estin*' (1 John 4, 8). Love cannot exist without distinct persons between whom love is given, received, and shared. So in God there must be a person who loves, a person who is loved, and perhaps also a person who shares in their love (or alternatively, as Augustine put it, a 'third thing', the love which flows between them). If the Christian God is love, then God must be an inner communion of love, a society of perfectly loving persons, and that is the life of the Trinity.

I can feel the attraction of this view. Perhaps a society of loving persons is more perfect than a self-contemplating and unchanging consciousness. Perhaps it puts before us an ideal which is essentially communal or social, rather than being more isolated and purely self-contained. So it can lead us to put a greater value on community and other-regarding love, and not so much value on a life of solitary, even rather self-satisfied, contemplation.

The 'social Trinity' view, as it is often called, also has the attraction that it is somewhat simpler for contemporary people to understand than the Athanasian Creed. However, I think it only seems simpler at first sight. In fact it may raise problems about how God can be both one and three, which are worse than those of more traditional formulations. I will be raising some of these problems myself.

CHAPTER 2

Why We May Need to Restate the Ways in Which We Talk about the Trinity

Perhaps it is important at this point to say that when I raise problems I am not meaning to undermine the point and profundity of Christian belief in God as Trinity. Quite the opposite – I am seeking a way of bringing out the profoundness and spiritual relevance of Trinitarian belief for the modern world. The problems I will discuss are problems of finding ways of saying things which are at the very limits of human comprehension – which are, as the Athanasian Creed puts it, 'incomprehensible'.

Of course, if something is completely incomprehensible it is just nonsense. But for most of us there are many things that we are unable to comprehend even though someone else may have a pretty good grasp of them. For instance, the Schrödinger equation, as used in quantum physics, is something that many of us just cannot understand. We can learn it, we can see that it is used, but we just cannot really see what it means. It is quite possible to see that an equation is useful, even to learn to repeat it and to see roughly how it works, yet fail to understand it.

An even better example would be the wave-particle duality of light. I think I am safe in saying that no one can understand how light can behave both in wave-like and in particle-like ways (in John Wheeler's 'delayed choice' version of the two-slit experiment, for example). There is no doubt, however, that it does, and various models have been invented to try to explain the mystery of it. We can see that there are good reasons for positing such a duality. What we cannot see is what sort of objective reality can account for the duality – though we assume that there *is* such a reality.

By analogy, we might see that there are good reasons for referring to God variously as Father, Son, and Spirit, and for insisting that there is just one God. But we might not be able to understand the sort of objective reality which would account for the appropriateness of our linguistic references. If this sort of analogy holds, we see how we could say that we cannot understand the reality of God, as it is in itself, but that we can see the appropriateness, perhaps the necessity, of referring to God, perhaps for different purposes, as both one and three.

There are three main reasons we may wish to revise the ways in which we talk about the Trinity. Firstly, when I talk about problems in the use of Trinitarian language, I am doing precisely that – talking about our uses of language, not directly about the objective reality of God. I am seeking an appropriate way for us in our historical situation, with the knowledge we have and with the language we have learned, to speak of divine reality. Since this reality is not a finite thing, but the creator of the whole cosmos, it is most unlikely that we can get a very clear grasp of it.

I am writing in twenty-first-century English, and the meanings English words have for me are very different from words in Latin or Greek from fifteen hundred years and more ago. That is why the words of the Athanasian Creed sometimes do not mean much to us. That is just not the way we speak any more. The paradox is that the more we try to say the same thing as people thought hundreds of years ago, the more we might have to change the words from the ones they actually used. The meanings of those words will have changed, and we need to find out what underlay the words they used and how that can be expressed in the very different language of today. For instance, in the Athanasian Creed we say that God is 'three persons in one substance'. But the words 'person' and 'substance' were originally in Greek and Latin and had quite different meanings at that time and in those languages than the English words mean today. So any modern English-speaker might use those words and mean something quite different from what the early theologians of the Church had in mind. That is, of course, why there are so many different translations of the Bible. We probably need new ways of translating words from ancient languages, bearing in mind that the possibilities for misunderstanding are numerous. Too many debates in religion are squabbles over words, just because people use the same words in different ways, or use very different words, often in different languages, to mean very similar things.

Secondly, we might want to change some of the things we say about God anyway. Probably – through decades of debate, argument, discussion, and reflection – we have come to think different things about God. A good example would be the belief that God is completely without change. Aristotle certainly thought this, and the belief passed into most Christian theological thinking about God, almost as an axiom. If God is perfect, it was thought, God will not need to, and will not, change.

But that belief is in tension with the belief that 'the Word became flesh', '*ho logos sarx egeneto*' (John 1, 14). And the Bible certainly seems to suggest that God changes: God is said to speak to Abraham and to Moses, to listen to what they have to say, and even to change his mind when he hears what they say. Belief that God is wholly changeless is not clearly attested in the Bible, is hard to reconcile with asking God for things, and is based more on Greek philosophical thought than on revelation.

I will be saying much more about this topic later, and I just want to signal at this stage that the idea of God can be interpreted in different ways. If what we say about God is based partly on philosophical reflection, rather than on a direct and clear revelation, we will probably modify what we say if and when we modify our philosophy. It is no accident that theologians who adopt an Aristotelian philosophy (modified by Thomas Aquinas) will stress the utter changelessness of God, whereas theologians who reject that philosophy may think it obvious that the God of Abraham, Isaac, and Jacob changes in response to what humans think and do – and adapt their idea of God accordingly.

It is consequently very important to ask how far our view of God depends upon a particular philosophy, how much importance we give to the truth of that philosophy, and how this may affect the account we give of the Trinity. For example, a Trinitarian God who is completely changeless will be spoken of very differently than a Trinitarian God whose members are capable of change as they relate to one another. That is part of the difference between classical Trinitarian and social Trinitarian accounts. It is, I think, basically a philosophical difference.

Thirdly, our view of the universe is markedly different from what people believed in Biblical times. We see the universe as hugely bigger in both space and time. Earth is just one small planet in a hundred thousand million star systems, in a middle-sized galaxy amid a hundred thousand million galaxies, in a universe which is perhaps one of billions of universes. That is very different from the Biblical view that the universe consisted of the earth at the centre, as a flat disc floating on water, and that the stars were lamps hung on the bowl of the sky.

Most scientists also see the universe as having evolved over about fourteen hundred thousand million years from a point of infinite density and mass (the 'Big Bang') to its present complex state. The universe will continue to exist for billions of years, and maybe cosmic evolution will continue in ways we can scarcely imagine. The destruction of the earth, while it is certain at some point, probably in the far future, will almost be irrelevant to this larger cosmic story. This too is a huge contrast with the Biblical view that the whole universe (that is, basically, the earth) came into existence about six thousand years ago, and may end at any moment.

For anyone who takes science seriously, this means that the context of Christian faith has changed completely since its origin. How far this may affect views of the Trinity remains to be seen. But it will certainly affect how we must interpret the Incarnation of the 'second person' of the Trinity as a human on earth. However much we may value past traditions, there will be specific respects in which we have to change our ways of putting things. How important, and how extensive, such changes might be is hard to know.

For some people, they may make Christian faith irrelevant. I believe that position to be too hasty and harsh a judgment. But for all the aforementioned reasons, there is a need to restate the doctrine of the Trinity in a twenty-first-century context. I would like to do so while preserving, and even reinforcing, the basic claims of Trinitarian faith. Those claims, however, will need to be reformulated in the context of greatly expanded knowledge of the universe and in the light of the changing history of philosophical ideas.

CHAPTER 3

The Doctrine of Divine Simplicity

Anyone who thinks about God as Trinity must keep firmly in mind the statement that Mark's Gospel attributes to Jesus: 'The first of all the commandments is, "Hear, O Israel; the Lord our God is one Lord"' (Mark 12, 29). Christians need to be clear that the most important commandment in the Bible, therefore, is that there is one and only one God. There are not three Gods, and nothing must be said which suggests that there are. That must be the starting point.

How, then, does talk of a Trinity arise? It is worth pointing out that even the strictest monotheists may use many different terms to refer to the one God. The most rigorous Muslims accept that there are ninety-nine beautiful names of God, even though they often interpret the Arabic word *tawhid*, oneness, as forbidding any plurality within God. Hindus, who are sometimes alleged to worship many Gods, often quote the Scriptural verse, from the Veda, that 'God is one, but has many names'. And many Jews, especially Kabbalistic Jews, are happy to say that there are many 'emanations' – or almost personalised properties (it is hard to find the right word) – of God, including such things as Wisdom, Power, and Spirit.

If God is in some sense infinite, it is hardly surprising that humans cannot just find one word which adequately describes God. We think of God in many ways, and perhaps we have to do so if we are to get anywhere near an understanding of divine reality.

Thomas Aquinas puts the point well: we must think of God as wise, good, and beautiful, and though these terms do not apply to God as we understand them, in some sense God really is wise, good, and beautiful (Aquinas, *Summa Theologiae*, 1a, Question 13).

These facts do not lead at once to a doctrine of the Trinity. Why should these different ways in which humans may speak of God be limited to three? And are these just 'ways of speaking', or do they correspond to something real in God?

When we ascribe a number to a thing or a class of things, it is imperative that we have an idea of the sort of thing we are talking about. If, for instance, I say, 'There is just one thing in this room', before you can make sense of that statement you have to have some idea of what I mean by a 'thing'. There might be one piece of furniture. But there would also be billions of atoms, lots of oxygen, and perhaps some windows too. The number always qualifies a specific sort of thing. So what I would really need to say would be something like 'There is just one medium-sized physical object in this room'. The less I can specify what sort of thing I am referring to, the less my statement communicates to a neutral observer.

In a similar way, if I say, 'There is just one God', I might well mean, 'There is just one creator of everything other than itself'. We could then ask in a meaningful way whether this is true or not. I think virtually all Jews, Muslims, and Christians would think it is true.

I might then ask, 'Are there a number of different properties which most people think of God as having?' I think there would be wide agreement that there are. In most theistic traditions, it would be more wrong to deny that God knows and wills and feels beatitude than to affirm that God does have these attributes.

This would mean that there is a certain sort of plurality in God. God's knowing is different from God's willing and from God's feeling. These are different attributes of the one God. But just at this point Aquinas would assert that in God they are not different. They are one and the same thing, even though in our limited human way we think of them as different. That is one meaning of divine 'simplicity'.

But why should Aquinas say this? It does not compromise the unity of God to say that God thinks, feels, and wills. In fact it supports the idea that there is just one God to say that it is the same God who thinks, feels, and wills. There are not, after all, different beings who do these things. This is one main reason I am uneasy about saying that God is a 'society' of three beings who think, feel, and will. That seems to undermine the belief that there is just one God – but of course this depends on exactly how you define 'God'.

Perhaps there is an internal complexity in the one and only God. Let me say that this supposition is not intended to get to the Trinity by a very short route. But it might open us up to the idea that certain sorts of complexity in God are perfectly harmless, or even logically necessary. If we can establish this, we can go on to ask if the Trinity is a sort of internal complexity in God. I am going to argue that it is.

At the beginning of his great work the *Summa Theologiae*, Thomas Aquinas spends some time defending the doctrine of divine simplicity. We might at once think that a Christian who believes that God is three in one can hardly also think that God is logically simple – in other words has no internal complexity at all. But Aquinas does. What forces him to such a paradoxical suggestion?

I think the idea of divine simplicity is not a revealed or Biblically grounded supposition. It follows from a certain sort of philosophical demand that God must be a complete explanation for everything (including even the divine being itself). I sympathise with that demand, while accepting that it is not a demand which weighs very heavily with most Christian believers. It is perfectly coherent to think that God explains why the universe exists (e.g. because God thinks it is good and chooses to create it), even though you cannot explain why God chose this exact universe, or why God is the way God is, or why God created anything at all. You can say that such things are beyond human comprehension or even that there is no answer to such questions, nothing to comprehend. That is just the way things are. The philosopher Richard Swinburne takes this line, holding that God is just the ultimate brute fact and does not stand in need of, and can logically never have, a further explanation. He is quite right in saying that such a God could explain the universe in a satisfactory way. Perhaps all explanations have to stop somewhere, and Swinburne argues that this would be a very simple and elegant place at which to stop. I suspect that many Christians would agree with him and leave it at that. Such a view, of course, does not require internal divine simplicity at all. It just requires that an internally complex God could be a simple explanation of why the universe exists. There is nothing incoherent about that.

But someone may ask for more. They may ask for an explanation of why God has the nature God has, an explanation of why God is complex in just the way God is, an explanation of why God exists, and an explanation of the cause of change (of why, perhaps, God decides to create a universe). I have taken these questions from a Roman Catholic theologian, Edward Feser, who thinks that only belief in divine simplicity will enable them to be answered satisfactorily. I want to show that they can best be answered, in fact, by positing divine internal complexity.

I am sympathetic to Feser's demands. I would find it very satisfying if even the existence of God had a convincing explanation. But how could asserting that God is simple, that 'there is no way in which God is composite' (*Summa Theologiae* 1a, 3, 7), function as an explanation? It would have to be an explanation of why absolutely everything in the universe is the way it is and why God is the way God is. Yet it seems vastly implausible to assert that something totally simple could explain how such vast complexity exists. Aquinas proposes that only the changeless explains change. But how could an unchanging thing explain that and why changes exist?

I am not denying that the changing could originate from the changeless. But what explains why or how it does so originate? Can we even understand how a changeless being could originate change? This is like asking why God creates a universe, and this universe in particular. But there does not seem to be any possible explanation for that. You could say, 'God just chooses to create', and that might be true. But why does God choose just this? Well, you might say, because it is good. But does God have to do it? If not, if God has a choice, then can you explain which choice God makes? The usual – and in the end I believe the correct – reply is that God just chooses out of divine freedom.

But look what is happening here. This is a sort of explanation. You are saying that the universe does not come into being for no reason, just by pure chance. It is chosen for the sake of its goodness by an omniscient mind. This explanation has important consequences. It means that the universe is good, or contains great goods, that it has a purpose, which is to realise those goods, and that events happen for a reason, not haphazardly.

This is a good explanation (even though many people would deny that it is correct). But it leaves some things unexplained. Why did God make just this free choice, out of all the other things God might have chosen?

If you say, 'Because God had to', then freedom disappears. But if you say, 'God's choice was free', then the possibility of a total explanation disappears. In the latter case, what you are really saying is that truly creative choices cannot be totally explained, either in terms of general laws or in terms of overwhelming values. It is not a pity that they cannot be totally explained. It is actually a good thing, because what you might be wanting, and what perhaps you should not be wanting from a total explanation, is something that determines what must happen. And it is precisely being denied that anything *determines* what must happen in every case and in every detail. It is being said that free creativity is a positively good thing, without which the universe would be much worse and God would be much worse.

Creativity is not chance, for it is directed towards goodness by intelligence. But its existence entails that there are many forms of goodness, that intelligence has many courses of action open to it, and that there are many forms of goodness between which God could freely choose. It entails that total (i.e. deterministic) explanation is factually impossible and morally questionable.

Why, then, does God have the nature God has? There is a reason: because without that nature there would be no creative freedom, and because such freedom is a great good and as such must be part of a divine nature which is of supreme goodness. In the Christian faith, a key belief is that 'God is love' (1 John 4, 8). It is not just that God is creatively free and supremely good. God's creative freedom is the freedom of love, and God's goodness is gracious relation to others in compassionate and cooperative ways. Here we uncover the basic difference between classical, purely 'cosmological' forms of explanation and what might be called more axiological forms of explanation – explanations in terms of value. When Thomas, in his first three ways of demonstrating the divine existence, following Aristotle, asks what explains a thing, he is asking for a necessary (ineliminable) cause. When someone asks what explains a thing axiologically, that person is asking for a supremely great value. So a cosmological explanation for why God has the nature God has will be in terms of necessity – it has to be that way. But an axiological explanation will be in terms of value: God instantiates in the divine being the greatest possible value – the value of creative love – and whatever God creates will be for the sake of some otherwise unobtainable value or form of love.

CHAPTER 4

Cosmological and Axiological Explanation

This raises the possibility that we could have both the greatest possible intelligibility and the greatest possible goodness. We could combine these forms of explanation and posit a being which is both necessary and of supreme goodness. It turns out that we can do just that. But there is a price that traditional Thomists are not usually prepared to pay. The price is this: if supreme goodness includes free creativity, and if God is necessarily freely creative, then it is necessarily true that God is not necessary in all respects. God will be both necessary and free. This is a perfectly coherent supposition, but only if there are some respects in which God is necessary and others in which God is free. This in turn entails that God is internally complex, having some necessary (fully determined) properties and some creatively free (not fully determined) properties.

This argument can be set out formally as follows:

1. A necessary truth is a truth that could not be, or have been, otherwise (definition).
2. A contingent truth is a truth that could be, or could have been, otherwise (definition).
3. No contingent truth can be derived from a necessary truth alone (axiom).
4. The cause of a contingent event must be contingent, since such an event might not have existed, and thus its cause might not have existed or might not have caused it (from 2 and 3).

5. Whatever knows a contingent event must be contingent, since such an event might not have existed, and thus knowledge of it might not have existed (from 2 and 3).
6. God exists by necessity (usually held by classical theists).
7. The universe is contingent, at least in part: it could have been different or might not have existed – God did not have to create this universe in particular, or maybe any universe.
8. Therefore God as creator of this universe must act contingently (from 4 and 7).
9. And God as omniscient knower of this universe must include contingent epistemic states (from 5 and 7).
10. Therefore God is not simple: God, while being necessary, does some things contingently and so is necessary in some respects and contingent in other respects (from 6, 8, and 9).

This conclusion can only be avoided if God is said to be not necessary (if God could have been otherwise, or might not have existed), or if the universe is said to be wholly necessary (if nothing in the universe could have been otherwise in any respect, or if the universe could not fail to exist). The problem is that most classical theists say that God did not have to create the universe (the universe is contingent) but that God is both necessary and simple (non-complex).

It seems a perfectly coherent supposition that a God who has to exist and has the general nature God has (say, of being the most powerful being possible and having the greatest possible knowledge and being the best possible being) might yet act in particular contingent ways. We can think of the set of all possible states of affairs, a set which is necessary (anything that is possible is necessarily possible). In this respect, God's knowledge of all possible universes will be necessary. God's evaluation of the goodness or desirability of these possible universes will also be necessary (their goodness or intrinsic worthwhileness is objective and not arbitrarily assigned to them by God). But God's decision to create a specific universe is contingent. God does not have to create this universe. God's creation is a free, not a necessary, act.

Such a God is complex. In a way, we might even say that there is a sort of Trinitarian idea of God in this conception already, though of course we are not yet approaching the Christian Trinity. The idea might be that in God there is a necessary knowledge of all possibles, a necessary 'feeling' or sensitivity to their value or disvalue, and a necessary ability to create (to make some possible states actual). There would be one mind, with three basic capacities of knowledge, feeling, and will. Augustine actually uses a model very like this one as a way of understanding the Trinity.

I think we can see how people might imagine a threefold God even apart from any Christian belief. We might speak, as some Hindus do, of God as creator (*Brahma*), preserver (*Vishnu*), and destroyer (*Siva*), and these may be seen as three personified aspects of one spiritual reality, *Brahman*, or the Absolute.

The neo-Platonist and non-Christian philosopher Plotinus also saw the Supreme as a Triad, consisting of 'the One', *Nous* or Intellect, and the World-Soul. Intellect and World-Soul emanate from, and have their source in, the One, and together they form a Divine Triad or Trinity. Even Buddhists in some schools have a doctrine not totally unlike this. They speak of the *Dharmakaya*, or eternal 'cosmic body', of the Buddha; the *Sambhogikakaya*, or glorified body of the Buddha, seated on a lotus throne in a Pure Land; and the *nirmanikakaya*, the earthly person of Siddhartha Gautama and of other manifestations of the Buddha on the physical plane.

I am certainly not saying that these are exactly like the Christian Trinity. My point is only that adherents of many traditions find various ways of speaking of an internal complexity within one God, or supreme spiritual reality. I have argued that anyone who thinks there is any contingency, any real freedom and creativity in the universe, but one creator of such a universe who necessarily exists with a nature of supreme value, is logically forced to speak of God as internally complex.

What lies behind Aquinas' first three ways (the cosmological arguments) is the basic thought that the actual is prior to the merely possible: 'actual existence takes precedence of potential existence' (*Summa Theologiae* 1a, 3, 1). There cannot be any possibles without something actual. I agree with that intuition, and for that reason I am inclined to think that there must be an actual reality within which possibles exist. I construe this as a mind which has to exist if any possibles exist (as they necessarily do) and which is a personal Subject who necessarily conceives of all possible states.

Thomas does not do this, for he thinks that God transcends every category, including that of mind. I have no objection to saying that God in the divine being itself is wholly beyond human comprehension. I would point out, however, that this entails that we cannot say anything about it. The 'via negativa', taken to its furthest degree, means that everything we say about God is false, at least as we understand it.

That leaves a major problem: if there is something we cannot conceive, how can we assert some things about it (such as 'God is good') and deny others (such as 'God is bad')? How can we even say that this something is the creator of the universe, since 'creation' means 'bringing something about through knowledge and intention'? All theists who believe that God creates the universe agree that one can truly say this of God. Even if God also transcends our understanding, it is true to say that God wills to create and knows that God is creating, and it is false to say that God does not wish to create a universe and does not even know that a universe is being created. This entails that it is true to speak of God as knowing and willing – and in this sense as a Mind – even if it also is true that God's being transcends our understanding.

Of course, insofar as God wholly transcends our understanding, we can neither say that God is simple nor that God is complex. What we can and must say is that insofar as we can understand God, which is to think of God as creator of this and any other cosmos, it is correct for us to think of God as complex. I conclude that if we speak of God as the free creator of the universe, or as supremely loving, we must speak of God as internally complex. This does not entail a doctrine of the Trinity. But it is significant that in many religious traditions a sort of threefoldness is posited in the Ultimately Real. And this opens the way to seeing the divine being as basically threefold, for reasons that have yet to be explored.

CHAPTER 5

Divine Potentiality and Temporality

I now want to argue that a freely creative God of love must logically be a God who is temporal in some respects, because free creation entails choosing between alternative states, and choosing entails change from potency to actuality, and change entails a form of temporality. Love, as humans understand it, also involves conscious relationship and responsiveness to others, and if these others are changing, as humans are, this entails change in response to changes in them. Furthermore, causing free creative and self-developing beings to exist brings about great goods that could not otherwise exist and therefore is a good reason for creating a universe. So a complex and temporal God provides a good explanation for the existence of a universe such as ours. If this is true, the ground is prepared for positing a threefoldness in the being of God and for building up a view of this threefoldness which can provide a distinctive picture of the dynamic, creative, and loving relationship of God to the created order.

I will first argue for the existence of potentiality in God. When Thomas says that the actual takes precedence over the potential, he does not deny, but rather affirms, the existence of potential things. For if one thing takes precedence over another, then that other clearly exists. So there are potential things, and indeed virtually all created things have potentiality – states that they could manifest but do not yet manifest. However, theologians such as Aquinas say that since God is absolutely simple, there can be no potentiality in God. If there were, we would have to distinguish what is actual in God from what is potential. But if we cannot do that, then God must be, as Aquinas says, 'purely actual'. But that entails that God cannot do anything other than God does. It seems to me an odd definition of 'omnipotence' to say that though God is omnipotent, God is unable to do anything other than what God does (though the theologian Friedrich Schleiermacher bravely accepted this view). It seems better to say that a truly omnipotent being would be able to do infinitely many things that it has not and perhaps will not do. But this entails that such a being – and even the most powerful possible, yet maybe not completely omnipotent, being – would incorporate huge numbers of possibilities. It would be not purely actual, but omni-potential.

Thomas' mistake is to think that if every change is a move from potentiality to actuality, and if the actual takes precedence over the potential, then God cannot be potential in any respect. To put this formally:

1. No possible state can exist without a prior actual state.
2. All change involves a move from possible to actual.
3. Changes in God involve a move from a possible state in God to an actual state in God (from 2).
4. Thus if God changes, there are some possible states in God that are prior to actual states in God (from 2 and 3).
5. Therefore God cannot be the first cause of all change (from 1 and 4).

This argument is valid only if proposition 1 is interpreted to mean that every possible state must be preceded logically by an actual state of the same sort. Thomas probably interpreted it this way. But it does not have to be interpreted this way, and it makes more sense as an explanation of change if it is not so interpreted.

The first proposition should be read as saying that no merely possible state can exist without *some* prior actual state. To take an example Thomas uses more than once, fire is hot, and a hot fire must have a cause. But that cause does not have to be hot, much less as hot as a fire. If God conceives of a future state of hotness, that conception in the mind of God is actual only as a concept, not as a hot thing. The mind of God is actual but is not anything like a hot fire. And the capacity of God to make possible hotness actual is an actual capacity. It is actual, however, precisely as the possession of a potentiality. In other words, the sort of prior actuality that is God is an actuality of a sort which possesses many potentialities.

The denial of any potentiality in God follows, for Thomas, from his assertion that God is not a thing with a nature but is a pure existing nature or Form, indeed the Form of 'existence itself' (*Summa Theologiae*, 1a, 3, 4: *Est igitur Deus suum esse*). There can, he asserts, be no unactualised potentiality in an existent nature, because potentialities belong to substances, not natures.

The problems with this view are numerous and well known. It is by no means clear that the idea of an independently existing nature not instantiated in any particular thing makes sense. It is not clear that 'existence itself' is more than an abstraction, since it has been plausibly argued that there must always be something that exists, and it is not helpful to say that 'existence exists'. Further, since God, on Thomas' view, must somehow contain all possible properties 'in a higher manner', it seems that God will be the most complex possible thing, not the simplest. Worse still, if God is perfect and already contains the fullness of actuality, there does not seem to be any possible point in the existence of a material universe. Such a universe could add nothing to God, could not change God in any way, and would therefore seem only to add imperfection to perfection, which seems pointless.

I am not here claiming to refute the Thomist conception of God. But I do want to point out that it is a purely philosophical conception and must be evaluated as such, not as an item of definite revelation. And it is a very disputed and difficult notion, which weakens any claim that it provides the best explanation of why the universe exists.

There is another way of thinking of God. It is to accept one main claim of the Thomist cosmological argument: there has to be something uncaused, changeless, and necessary if the universe is to be truly intelligible. But we might want to add that there also has to be something which is free, creative, and contingent in the cause of the universe if the universe is to contain free, creative, and contingent elements.

There are good reasons for thinking that the universe known to modern science is open and emergent. That is, there are many alternative ways in which the universe could go, and new properties and values will emerge in it as it progressively develops, partly by the free choices of intelligent beings within it. In such a universe, creativity and freedom are great values. Such values, together with those of learning, striving, and cooperating – which will necessarily be involved in such a universe – could not exist at all unless there were emergent societies of creatively free agents.

This already suggests a form of explanation for the universe's existence. The explanation would be that having such a universe is a necessary condition of realising values of creative freedom, self-development, and cooperative relationship. Unless these values actually exist, they will merely be possibilities in the mind of God. Even as conceived possibilities, they may have great value for God. But if they are not actualised, they will have no value for other (created) persons, and God will have no knowledge of what goes on in the minds of those persons, since created persons will not exist as creatively free beings. In other words, the creation of an actual universe will make a difference to what sorts of values exist (it will add to the number and nature of values) and therefore also to God's knowledge of what values exist. As long as these values are sufficiently great, the creation of a universe will be good, but it does not have to be – and perhaps logically cannot be, if the choices of free creatures are taken into account – the one and only best possible universe.

This presupposes that possible universes exist in a divine mind that has the capacity freely to choose to actualise a specific set of values out of all those possibilities. The set of values and the mind which cognises them are necessary, whereas the actual choice to create is free and thus contingent. If this is a good explanation of the existence of a universe such as ours, then it is necessary that God, while being one subject of knowledge, experience, and action, is logically complex. God is simple, however, in the sense that God is not a combination of separate independent parts. God is one subject with many necessary properties, and among those properties there are some which entail that God is necessarily contingent in some respects. This is most clearly so when God is seen to be the creatively free creator of a universe from which emerge, by natural and inherent principles, societies of creatively free creatures.

If creativity and contingency are ascribed to God, it follows that God is in some sense temporal. That is, to put it in Aristotelian terms, in God there is movement from potentiality to actuality. There are alternative future possibilities for God, some of which come into being. So there is a divine time, which makes creative change and contingency possible. That time will not be measurable, and neither will it be identical with the time of this physical universe, which begins to be and will eventually cease to be. But it marks a great change in human ideas of perfection to think that creativity and change are perfections, not imperfections, and that it would be an imperfection in a being of supreme value not to be able to do new things and not to be able to respond in new ways to the acts of free and created beings. The Christian beliefs that this universe did not have to exist and that God freely chose to become embodied within it most naturally suggest a temporally involved view of God. If it had not been for the overwhelming influence of Plato on the course of Western philosophy, the 'simple, changeless, and timeless' view of supreme perfection might never have existed.

The American theologian Robert Jenson provides a more Biblically based argument for the temporality of the Christian God, who is the redeemer of humanity as well as the creator of all things. Jenson rejects a 'Hellenic' doctrine of God as timeless and impassible, in favour of a 'Gospel' salvation history which sees God as temporal and constantly changing in relation to the human temporal world. He writes, '"Begetting", "being begotten", "proceeding", and their variants are biblical terms for temporal structures of evangelical history, which theology ... then uses for relations said to be constitutive of God's life' (Jenson, 1982, p. 106). Patristic theology developed the view that God is simple and changeless, these being divine perfections. For such a view, there is no 'internal history' of God, and there are no active, changing relations between the Trinitarian persons. This view does not easily cohere with claims that 'the Word became flesh', or that the Spirit works actively within human lives, or even that God freely created the cosmos, when God need not have done so. Heroic philosophical work was done to show how a purely changeless reality could generate a temporal reality, work within it, and unite it to the divine. But if we are to see the heart of Christianity as a hope for the union of creation with creator, a union of temporal and eternal, of finite and infinite, then it seems that in some sense temporality must be, or become, part of the being of God.

Jenson's point is that it is misleading to think of the intra-Trinitarian relations as changeless relations within a simple reality. For such relations are projections into an allegedly purely eternal reality of what in the New Testament are presented as historical events: God begetting Jesus as the divine Son and the Spirit proceeding into the world, most obviously at the first Pentecost. We should, he holds, stay with those historical acts and not read them into some purely internal features of an assumed eternal and pre-existing reality. I am persuaded that the most natural reading of the Biblical narratives is that the creator God actively relates and responds to human acts and decisions. It is very difficult to see how such a reading can be consistent with seeing God as wholly without complexity or change. So the way is open to develop a view of God as complex and relational. Construing God as Trinitarian is such a view.

What I have been attempting to establish is that the assertion of divine simplicity does not provide a wholly satisfactory explanation of why the created universe is as it is. There is a form of axiological explanation which entails that although God is simple in not being made up of separable parts, God must logically be complex in having what we must think of as differing aspects of the divine being – such as knowing, experiencing, and willing – and in being capable of creative change and responsive love.

When we speak of God as one, therefore, that does not preclude – in fact, I have argued that it implies – that there is an internal complexity in God or in the way we speak adequately of God. There are various ways of construing such complexity, though in a number of philosophical and religious traditions a basic threefold division has been found helpful. If this is so, it will not be initially absurd to speak of God as being threefold, within a more basic unity of being. This thought should lead us to think that it may well make sense to say that God is both one- and threefold, in different respects. But all this has just been preparing the conceptual ground for beginning to understand the Christian Trinity. For the Christian view has rather different, and non-philosophical, sources.

PART II

The Biblical Sources of Trinitarian Thought

CHAPTER 6

Three Centres of Consciousness?

The Christian doctrine of the Trinity does not have its main source in relatively abstract philosophical considerations, though its various formulations have been influenced by them. What chiefly generates the Christian view is reflection on the person of Jesus and his relation to the creator God. It is in the New Testament that the main material for such reflection is to be found, and it is to it that one must look for the earliest written sources of Christian beliefs about Jesus.

It is generally agreed that the New Testament does not contain a clear statement that God is a Trinity, certainly not in the sense that came to be defined in fourth- and fifth-century councils of the Church. Nowhere in the Gospels can we find a statement that God is three persons in one substance, all co-eternal and co-equal, and that Jesus is in some sense identical with one of them. Tertullian is generally taken to be the originator of the expression 'three persons in one substance' – *una substantia, tres personae*. Jesus never said, 'I am the second person of a co-eternal and co-equal Trinity', so this has to be taken as a later attempt to work out what was only implicit in Jesus' teachings and acts.

Nevertheless, some theologians find evidence of three distinct individuals, who are all divine (three subjects of consciousness and will – Father, Son, and Spirit), in the Gospels. This is by no means an absurd suggestion. Indeed, it has much to commend it. Jurgen

Moltmann points out that Jesus, as recorded in the Synoptic Gospels, usually refers to God as his 'father'. This already makes a distinction between God the Father and Jesus. They are obviously not the same thing. Jesus prays to the Father, and he is not just praying to himself. In John's Gospel, Jesus says that 'I came from the Father . . . and am going to the Father' (John 16, 28). He prays, 'Father, the hour has come; glorify your Son' (John 17, 1). The Father 'sends' his Son into the world, and Jesus says, 'The Father is greater than I' (John 14, 28), which seems to emphasise the difference between Father and Son. In the Synoptic Gospels, too, a distinction is made between Jesus and the Father. At Jesus' baptism, a voice from heaven says, 'This is my beloved Son' (Mark 9, 7). The Son is an object of the Father's love, and surely the Father is not simply loving himself, albeit in human form. In Gethsemane Jesus prays, 'My Father, if it is possible, let this cup pass from me; yet not what I want but what you want' (Matthew 26, 39). And on the cross he cries out, 'My God, my God, why have you forsaken me?' (Matthew 27, 46). The Father and the Son are spoken of as if they could have different desires, which implies that they have different centres of consciousness. And the difference is so great that one may even be said to forsake the other. Given that Jesus is granted divine status in the Gospels, it looks as though there are at least two divine individuals who converse with one another.

It is more difficult to find statements in the Synoptic Gospels that the Spirit is a distinct centre of consciousness, but John's Gospel states that Jesus sends the Spirit to the disciples (John 16, 7) or, in an alternative formulation, that the Father sends the Spirit at the request of Jesus (John 14, 16), which implies that the Spirit is different from Jesus and from the Father. The Spirit will guide the disciples into all truth (John 16, 13). Guiding (or 'teaching' in John

14, 26) is typically something persons do. Romans 8, 26 affirms that 'the Spirit intercedes with sighs' for the saints, and Ephesians 4, 30 calls on the faithful not to 'grieve the Holy Spirit'. 'Interceding', 'sighing', and 'grieving' are personal verbs, and so it seems natural to think that the Spirit is a third divine person or centre of consciousness. Moltmann concludes that there are three divine individuals who are reciprocally conscious of one another and who communicate with one another.

The American philosopher and theologian William Hasker similarly claims that if the Son was not clearly distinguished from the Father as a separate person, then when the Bible records Jesus as praying to the Father, we would have to say that God would be 'praying to himself, talking to himself, and answering himself – indeed, crying out to himself in anguished protest for having forsaken himself' (Hasker, 2013, p. 188).

Wolfhart Pannenberg also makes much of the fact that in the Gospels Jesus seems to address God as another, and he takes this distinction into the inner life of the Trinity: 'As God reveals himself, so he is in his eternal deity' (Pannenberg, 1992, p. 300). If Jesus truly reveals God, and distinguishes himself from the Father, then that distinction is constitutive of the Trinity. Jesus and the Father are distinct persons – 'not merely as different modes of being of the one divine subject but as living realisations of separate centres of action' (Pannenberg, 1992, p. 319). Pannenberg even takes issue with the traditional view that the Father alone is the source of the other two persons of the Trinity, holding that the Father cannot exist without the other divine persons and that only together do those persons constitute God. Taking the Holy Spirit into account as well, Pannenberg also maintains that in God there are three separate centres of action and consciousness, three 'persons' almost in the modern sense of conscious subjects.

The Biblical case for a social Trinity may seem decisive. But it has its problems. The three centres of consciousness do not seem to be equal persons. It is the Father who commands, who sends, and who ultimately controls. The Son's role is to ask, to hear, and to obey the Father's will, not to initiate any independently chosen courses of action. And the Spirit seems to be almost entirely passive, carrying out what he is sent to do but not apparently taking any part in a divine conversation about what is to happen. Indeed, the Spirit is sometimes described as if he was a sort of impersonal force or power which causes Jesus to be conceived in Mary's womb, by which Jesus casts out demons (Matthew 12, 28), and which Jesus 'sends upon' the disciples (Luke 24, 49), rather than being a fully conscious person. The Father commands, the Son executes, and the Spirit witnesses, empowers, and brings to mind what was done. If these are three individuals, there seems to be a clear hierarchical line of authority between them, which makes any thought that they are three fully individual persons who are equal with one another dubious.

There is a much greater problem when consideration is given to the human consciousness of Jesus. If, as the later Chalcedonian definition would assert, Jesus is 'truly human', then his human consciousness would have to be very different from the divine consciousness. As the classical Christian idea of God developed, it saw divine consciousness as simple, eternal, and impassible. God would know all things from the beginning to the end of time in one supra-temporal vision, and in detail. God would not be changed at all by anything that occurred in time, and God would not even have real temporal relations to anything in time, since God does not exist in time. Any truly human consciousness, however, will gain knowledge primarily through sense-experience and by being taught by other humans. Its knowledge will develop and be largely dependent upon the culture and beliefs of its time; it will develop and suffer inevitable limitations; it cannot be omniscient or omnipotent. That Jesus' human consciousness involved suffering and dying is of critical importance to the Christian faith. But an impassible God is incapable of suffering.

In what was to become Patristic orthodoxy, it was asserted that the human consciousness of Jesus was identical with the divine consciousness of the eternal Logos. Indeed, it was widely held that the only subject of Jesus' human experiences *was* the divine Logos.

This, however, is logically impossible, as a short argument shows:

1. The divine is changeless and timeless and impassible.
2. The Logos is divine.
3. The Logos is changeless, timeless, and impassible (from 1 and 2).
4. The human Jesus is changing, temporal, and subject to suffering.
5. Therefore the human Jesus cannot be identical with the Logos (from 3 and 4).

This argument is easily countered by just denying the first premiss, and I have done precisely that in the first section of this book. Then we might say that the temporal experiences of Jesus, including his sufferings, are assimilated into the experience of the divine Word. Further, the divine Word could enter into a temporal existence, acting in and through the person of Jesus. We would be departing from Patristic orthodoxy here, but not, I think, in a fundamental way. The aim is the same: to see how a human being could be identical with the divine being. I think that including a human experience in the divine experience, and allowing a divine agent to act in time through a human agent, is a more coherent way of explaining such an identity than simply asserting that a temporal experience is identical with an eternal experience – though both are completely different in content.

Even so, Christian tradition asserts that there is one 'person', one identical individual, who has two completely different forms of consciousness and will. There is the limited human consciousness of Jesus and the presumably almighty and omniscient consciousness of the eternal Word. They are not thought of as two distinct individual subjects, but as two aspects of one subject indissolubly bound together. As Thomas Morris puts it in his rigorous analysis of the Incarnation, one 'mind' has complete knowledge of and control over the other, though it could allow the other (the human mind) a degree of access to the divine mind and of creative autonomy (Morris, 1986). It follows that there can be more than one subject of consciousness and will existing within the same individual existent. I do not think that this 'two minds' view is ultimately satisfactory, and I will later provide a different account. But it seems to be a logically coherent account, and it gives a persuasive contemporary reworking of what the Patristic writers formulated in a different philosophical milieu. One intriguing possibility is that the model could be extended to give a rather different account of the relations of the Trinitarian persons than 'three distinct individuals'.

It remains to be explained how the experience of Jesus could be uniquely assimilated into the experience of the Word, when the Word, as omniscient, would have intimate knowledge of all human experiences anyway. The New Testament suggests that the experience of Jesus is unique in that in Jesus we have one who 'has been tested as we are, yet without sin' (Hebrews 4, 15). There is no alienation between the man Jesus and the Word of God, so there is no moral dissonance between human and divine. This is because the Word from the first moment of Jesus' existence so fills the life of Jesus that no dissonance can arise. We could say, with the Patristic writers, that the Word is the true subject of Jesus' experiences, though I would add that Jesus is also a truly human subject of experiences, a human consciousness which is assumed without any 'moral distancing' into the divine experience.

It is also important to see how the omnipotent Word could act in Jesus without Jesus becoming a mere puppet, without real personal freedom and creativity. It cannot be that there is no human subject in Jesus, which would make him less than fully human. Rather, the human subject is so suffused or saturated with the divine subject that any opposition to the divine will becomes unthinkable. It does not mean that there is no creative agency in Jesus. This means that his actions always mediate the divine will, even though they may express that will in particular ways which are creatively free. Jesus' will is always for good, though there are many particular ways in which forms of goodness can be created and expressed.

Given these facts, Jesus can be a fully human subject who has a unique and indissoluble unity with the divine Word. The eternal Word is expressed in him in the fullest way that is possible in a human life, and he contributes to the Word the experiences of human relationship and suffering that could only exist by the real participation of the divine in time. By this reasoning, the Patristic view that the Word is the subject of Jesus' experiences and acts is not simply being rejected; it is being supplemented by an acceptance that if Jesus is to be truly human, he must be a human subject of experience and action. There is really no such thing as a 'truly human nature' that is possessed only by a divine subject without being a human subject. What is being rejected is the Patristic view that the divine nature is essentially changeless and impassible – a purely Greek philosophical postulate that fails to reflect the dynamic and strongly relational presentation of God in the Bible. So the unity of human subject and divine Word consists in the fact that the human experience is included and accepted into (owned and acknowledged by) the divine experience, and the divine character and intentions are expressed without distortion in the free, creative actions of the human agent. For Christians, this is uniquely, fully, and indissolubly the case only in Jesus.

Starting from the Patristic formulation that the Word is the subject of Jesus' experiences, it is easy to move to the conclusion that it is the Word who prays to the Father and that this establishes a relationship of two personal individuals within the being of God itself. But this does not quite seem to be what the New Testament writings imply. When Jesus, in his human nature, prays to the divine nature of the Father, he acknowledges that the divine nature is 'greater' than his human nature and that the will of the Father, without which nothing can exist, is superior to his own human will, which is limited and wholly dependent upon that of the Father. It is Jesus who prays to the Father, not the Father who prays to the Son. Praying, after all, is not conversation; it is, or includes, requests addressed to a being of infinitely greater power. So while the fact that Jesus prays to the Father distinguishes Jesus from the Father, it does not seem to reflect a distinction between two persons of the same sort.

It is Jesus as a dependent human being who prays to a being of much greater power who has ultimate control over the whole universe. In other words, the Biblical relationship between Father and Son is depicted as a relation between a limited and dependent human being and an almighty creator, even though that human being is identified with the divine in a way that is not explained. Prayer in this context is not straightforwardly a conversation between two almighty individuals (the eternal Father and Son). Even if the Word is the ultimate subject of Jesus' acts, it is the suffering and limited human subject, included in the Word though it is, who prays to the Creator. There is a relationship here; truly, Jesus does not pray to himself. But the relationship is extremely hard to characterise. In John's Gospel,

Jesus says, 'The words I say to you I do not speak on my own; but the Father who dwells in me does his works' (John 14, 10). It is a relationship of complete dependence on Jesus' part and complete authority on the Father's part.

Jesus could express and incarnate the eternal wisdom of God in human form, and in that sense he would be God the Word. But as human he prays to that same God insofar as God is also the omniscient and almighty ordainer of the cosmos. In other words, the human who is the embodiment and expression of the divine Word prays to the Mind which generates the Word and creates and sustains the cosmos. Jesus is praying to the same God that he himself expresses in human form; but that is not the same as 'praying to himself'.

The relationship of the Spirit to Father and Son also does not seem to be in any straightforward way a relationship of distinct individuals. The Spirit lives 'in' the disciples (John 14, 17), whereas persons do not normally live in one another. The Spirit is sent either by the Father or by Jesus and has the specific job of guiding the disciples into truth, but he does not seem to have a will of his own: 'He will not speak on his own, but will speak whatever he hears' (John 16, 13). The Spirit is certainly active and causally effective. But is the Spirit a distinct person, with a will and experience of his own?

There are reasons to doubt a 'three individuals' view of the Trinity. The relation of Jesus to the Father seems to be that of a human consciousness to its divine source, and the identity of that human consciousness to the divine Word, even if it is asserted or implied, remains unclear, and certainly unique. This is not an ordinary relationship of two individuals of the same sort. Further, the Spirit does not seem to be a participant member of a group of three individuals who together decide upon what is to happen in the world, as Pannenberg seems to suggest. The Spirit sometimes seems more like a power (Pannenberg himself even describes Spirit as a 'field of force') that is at the disposal of the Father and the Son.

The truth is that no human concepts seem to exist that give a clear and comprehensive account of the matter – which probably points more to the inadequacy of human language than to something defective in reality itself. My conclusion is that while a 'social' account of the Trinitarian God has a basis in the Biblical writings, there are difficulties with it that might lead one to look for something different. In the chapters that follow, I will suggest that there is indeed a different interpretation which the texts permit.

CHAPTER 7

The Synoptic Gospels

I will begin my discussion of the Biblical texts with the Gospels. Although they are to be dated later than most of the Letters in the New Testament, they are the only records we have of the life and teachings of Jesus. As such, they have special importance in the search to understand the relation between Jesus, God the Father, and the Spirit of God. Do the Synoptic Gospels really imply that God, Jesus, and the Spirit are three centres of consciousness? New Testament scholars would be very wary of reading later Christian doctrines or perspectives back into the Scriptural texts, and they are much more likely to stress the great diversity of views that exists in the texts, as well as the relatively undeveloped character of those views.

There would be agreement that early Christian communities were committed to the worship of one creator God. Those communities found that in relating to the risen and glorified Jesus, they were in some way relating to God. And they believed that God was present within and among them as the Spirit of Jesus. It was this experience of a threefold manifestation of God that was to lead to the development of Trinitarian thought. But there is not much agreement about what exactly might be said of the historical Jesus and his precise relation to the creator God.

Though the Gospels refer to him as 'son of God', Jesus, as he is depicted in the Gospels, does not usually refer to himself as 'Son of

God'. He more often refers to himself as 'Son of Man'. This expression, *Bar Nasha* in Aramaic, means, as Geza Vermes points out, the son of a human, and so a human person. Jesus was certainly believed to be a unique human being in many ways. He has authority to forgive sins, to exorcise evil spirits, and to control wind and sea. His life is a fulfilment of prophecies that he will be rejected, will suffer, and will die as a 'ransom for many' (Mark 10, 45). He was raised from death and will appear in 'the glory of his Father with the holy angels' (Mark 8, 38). This situation certainly puts this human in a very close relation to the Father and distinguishes Jesus from all other human persons. Yet however remarkable and unprecedented these things are, they do not detract from Jesus' real humanity, and that seems to be something that Jesus' use of the expression 'Son of Man' reinforces.

The phrase 'Son of Man' is, however, one of the most debated phrases in the New Testament. The major use of the expression 'Son of Man' in the Jewish Scriptures is Daniel chapter 7, verse 13. The context is that the prophet Daniel had a dream in which four great beasts came out of the sea. They are commonly taken to symbolise great imperial empires of the ancient world, tyrannical and militaristic rulers of the earth. Then God takes the throne, judges those world empires, and gives dominion to 'one like a son of man, coming with the clouds of heaven'. This Son of Man is given a kingship over all nations, and his kingdom will never be destroyed.

Norman Perrin argued that Jesus consciously used the expression 'Son of Man' with this passage of Daniel in mind. But Larry Hurtado agrees with Geza Vermes that the expression does not attribute a special character to the speaker. That is, it is not used as a title but is simply an admittedly unique form of self-reference, as if to say, 'This human being'. Nevertheless, it is hard to think that the

Daniel passage, as well as passages in the Major Prophets which refer to prophets as 'son of man', was not in Jesus' mind at all. Thus Hurtado writes, 'Jesus thought of himself as having a particular, probably even unique, divine vocation and mission ... [as] a particular mortal called to a special role in the coming of the kingdom of God' (Hurtado, 2011, p. 176).

There can be little serious doubt that the Gospel writers believed Jesus to have used the phrase 'the son of man' to refer to himself, and the fact that it is recorded, even though it dropped out of use very early in Christian history, suggests that it is an authentic memory. Even if the phrase does not in itself suggest any particular role for Jesus, the one who called himself 'the son of man' is depicted as having a very special relation to God. He was 'sent by God' (Mark 9, 37). In Luke's Gospel, he appears to identify the kingdom of God with his own kingdom: 'I appoint to you a king-dom, as my father has appointed me, that you may eat and drink at *my* table in *my* kingdom, and sit on thrones judging the twelve tribes' (Luke 22, 29; italics mine). Jesus sits in the place of God, or perhaps as God's human regent. His task is to call sinners to repentance and to proclaim that the kingdom 'has come near' (Mark 1, 15).

In Matthew 25, the Son of Man sits on the throne of his glory, all nations gather before him, and he separates just from unjust. It would be reasonable to note that a human being could not literally be the judge of all nations. Such judgment requires a complete knowledge of the inner thoughts of others, and there will be billions of others to take into account and for whom to find a fully just allocation of reward or punishment. An omniscient God could manage that, but no human being could have such time or ability. Can we even imagine a human person meeting every human who has ever lived and assessing their moral worth with perfect justice?

There would be billions of people to be assessed and billions of nuances in their inner lives to be brought to light and evaluated. That seems infinitely beyond any purely human capacity, however enlarged. Universal and perfectly just judgment is the sole prerogative of God.

This is clearly a picture or parable. But what does it picture? It must picture the infinite God, who understands human hearts fully and compassionately. It is not that there is literally a human figure on a throne, surrounded by angels. This Son of Man image, then, would not describe an individual human person, but would be a symbol of one who has achieved the moral goal of humanity. That the Son of Man sits on a throne and judges all nations we could take as a pictorial way of saying that all humans will be judged with perfect justice, by the standard of the ideal of humanity which is always in the mind of God and was expressed in the person of Jesus.

A Biblical analogy might be the Genesis account of Adam and Eve, in which God walked in the garden looking for them. Readers who believe that God is beyond any imaginable human form ('To whom will you liken me and make me equal, as though we were alike?' Isaiah 46, 5) know that there is not a divine being who has legs and walked in a garden and did not know where Adam and Eve were. This is more like a picture of the divine search for a humanity which was about to become estranged from God by self-will. I am not saying that there is one correct and final interpretation of the picture. The important point is that the picture must be interpreted, that there is more than one possible interpretation, and that it is misunderstood if it is taken as a literal description.

If this is accepted, the Judgment of the nations by the Son of Man takes on a new significance. For the Son of Man came to give his life as a ransom for many (Mark 10, 45). The Judge is also the Saviour.

That is what turns the fear of judgment into the hope of forgiveness and redemption. It is a Gospel of hope, not of fear.

The Son of Man, then, is one whose particular life expresses the universal judgment and redemption of God. Though Jesus is undoubtedly human, he is closely associated with God. This close association, as Larry Hurtado and others have argued, is in some sense an identification. For in the early Christian communities which the Gospels presuppose, Jesus was already worshipped along with God. However difficult this was for Jews, in the New Testament Epistles Jesus is addressed as *kyrios*, Lord, a term used for God. The Letter of 1 Corinthians 8, 5–6, for instance, says: 'For us there is one God, the Father . . . and one Lord, Jesus Christ, through whom are all things.' It cannot be said that the relation of the 'one God' and the 'one Lord' is clear. The created world seems to come from one God *through* the one Lord. In this and many other passages, the Lord seems to be both identical with the Father – yet also a seeming mediator between the Father and human beings – and a real human being.

The fact is that Jesus was worshipped as Lord in the early churches, and yet there were not two Gods. Moreover, Jesus was also human. According to the Biblical record, there are things the Son does not know – for instance, the time of the Kingdom's coming (Mark 13, 32). He 'increased in wisdom', according to Luke 2, 52, and so was not always perfectly wise. There are things he does not control – for instance, who is to sit on his right or left in the Kingdom (Mark 10, 40). And there are seemingly some things he does not will, though God the Father does will them – 'Not my will, but yours, be done' (Mark 14, 36). The will of Jesus is freely subordinated to the will of God, but they are different wills.

This, as outlined in the previous section, could be taken as a Biblical commitment to a sort of 'social Trinity'. Within the being

of God there is an individual agent, the Father, and another individual agent, the Son, who is worshipped as God and yet becomes
human. But the text is both more cryptic and more complex even
than that.

Jesus is a man sent and appointed by God to have supreme
authority and to rule over other humans in the coming Kingdom,
when he will sit at the right of God in glory and power. He is the
Messiah, the liberator and King, and the Lord of all people, who
are called to be his disciples. Such a person is in some sense both
human and divine, and there is indeed good reason here for
thinking of God as being at least twofold – both wholly transcendent to humanity and also united to humanity. The complication is
that the limitations, and especially the sufferings and death, of Jesus
are difficult to ascribe to God. So one cannot simply place Jesus, a
limited and suffering and dying person, alongside the creator God
as identical in every respect.

These are matters that were debated furiously in Patristic
theology, and the fact that such debates were serious and hotly
contested is proof enough that the Gospel texts were unclear. I
think, therefore, that the Synoptic Gospels give good reason for
beginning to think of God as Trinity. But they give no clear
guidance as to how it is that a man can be identified with God or
how humanity and divinity can be coherently united in the person
of Jesus. There is not a doctrine of a social Trinity in the Synoptic
Gospels.

Of course, if the Christian God is a Trinity, there must be a third
'person', the Holy Spirit. Remarkably little is said about the Spirit
in the Synoptic Gospels. The Spirit descended on Jesus at his
baptism by John (1, 10). So it seems that the Spirit of God is with
him in a special and unique way. But it must be said that the Spirit
often sounds rather like an impersonal power or force which can

descend on people or which can empower the lives of disciples, prophets, and poets (as it does throughout the Hebrew Scriptures). The Gospels of Matthew and Luke assert that Jesus was conceived by the Holy Spirit. This gives the Spirit a role as the giver of life, or perhaps as the power of God to give life. Again, the Gospel texts are vague enough to make many early Christians unsure whether the Spirit was divine or not. The Hebrew Bible speaks of the Spirit of God, and the question remains to be settled how far the connection of the Spirit with the life of Jesus means that the Hebrew understanding of the Spirit (and of course there are many such understandings) must be modified for Christians. I am not denying that it must be modified; I am only asserting that the Synoptic texts do not enable us to clearly declare that the Spirit is a distinct centre of consciousness within the being of God. It is not a question they ever raise.

There can be little doubt that even in the Synoptic Gospels Jesus is assumed to have divine status and authority. Matthew's Gospel opens with the angelic declaration that Jesus 'will save his people from their sins' (Matthew 1, 21). It does not say that Jesus will save the Jews from Roman oppression. He will 'save his people from their sins' – from the things that place a barrier between them and God. Only God, or possibly the one who is authorised to stand in the place of God, can save from sin. Jesus may be human, but he is seen as having divine authority and as acting on behalf of God. This puts Jesus' kingship and his rule at God's right hand in a distinctive light. It suggests that Jesus will not be a political ruler or one who exercises overwhelming power. He will be a healer and a reconciler between humanity and God, and one through whom God acts uniquely to liberate humans from sin. The actions of God are so intertwined with the actions of Jesus that it is possible to speak of God and Jesus together as *kyrios*.

Both Matthew and Luke include a phrase which has been called a 'Johannine thunderbolt' – namely, 'Only the Son knows the Father, and only the Father knows the Son' (Matthew 11, 27). That is because it is more typical of John than of the Synoptics to stress the absolute uniqueness of Jesus' knowledge of God and relationship to God as Father. Jesus knows the Father in a way that is not possible for anyone else. This is certainly a remarkable claim. Yet it still leaves completely unresolved the problem of just how to construe the relation between the human Jesus and God.

Matthew's Gospel concludes with the risen Christ's assertion (even if this is a later insertion, it records what was widely believed about Jesus in the early Church): 'All authority is given to me in heaven and earth' and the commission to baptise 'in the name of the Father, the Son, and the Holy Spirit' (Matthew 28, 18). Here, it may seem, is a clear statement of the Trinity at last. But what sort of Trinity is it? 'The Father' is certainly the creator of all, who sends the Son to do his will. The Son is sent to do the will of God, he prays to God, and he commends his spirit to God. He seems to be a human being who is raised to and clothed with divine glory, the glory of the Father, which the Father gives to him. The Spirit is the life-giving power which brings the human Jesus into being and rests on Jesus, as well as 'the power from on high' (Luke 24, 49) which Jesus sends out, or breathes onto, the disciples.

It would be a mistake to seek any sort of systematic doctrine here. In particular, it does not seem that any sort of 'social' doctrine of the Trinity can be found in these Gospels. The creative power of God, the unique relation of Jesus to God, and the life-giving power of the Spirit of God are all clearly asserted. But few conclusions can be drawn about their exact relations. There is nothing here which is in principle offensive to anyone who insists on the unity of God and accepts that the risen Jesus is worthy of worship but feels some reserve about speaking in detail of 'the inner life of God'. There may be great virtue in this, the virtue of a reverent reserve in presuming to speak about what God is really like. As some ancient rabbis said, 'We know what God commands, but not what God is'. It might be good for Christian theologians to practise such reserve.

CHAPTER 8

John's Gospel

It is in the fourth Gospel that we clearly see evidence of a marked development of thinking about the person of Jesus. The relation of the Prologue (John 1, 1–18) to the rest of the Gospel is much debated, and my own view is that the Prologue, even or perhaps especially if written later, can justly be taken as the key to interpreting the rest of the Gospel. The Prologue is now, anyway, part of the canonical text and can be taken as a genuine early reflection on the cosmic status of Jesus which became an important part of Christian tradition. It lives in a wholly different conceptual space from the other Gospels. It does not begin from the life of Jesus. It begins with God: 'In the beginning was the Word, and the Word was with God, and the Word was God' (1, 1). The phrase 'In the beginning' immediately echoes the first words of the Hebrew Bible: 'In the beginning God created . . .' That 'beginning' is the beginning of this universe, the beginning of this created cosmos. As such, it does not refer to the being of God in itself, beyond any actual created universe. It refers to the fact that this cosmos began and was brought into being by God. So, we might think, John is not referring to God beyond, and considered apart from, creation. John is referring to the origin of this cosmos and saying that at the origin of this cosmos the Word already was.

Because in the phrase 'The Word was God' the word *theos* is used without a definite article, many scholars hold that it should be translated 'The Word was divine', leaving the exact form of identity with God indeterminate. There are echoes of the Wisdom tradition here, especially perhaps in the Wisdom of Solomon chapter 7 and Proverbs chapter 8. The former says, 'She [wisdom] is a breath of the power of God, and a pure emanation of the glory of the Almighty . . . for she is a reflection of eternal light, a spotless mirror of the working of God, and an image of his goodness' (Solomon 7, 25–26). And the latter says, 'When he [God] marked out the foundations of the earth, then I was beside him, like a master worker [or little child]; and I was daily his delight, rejoicing before him always' (Proverbs 8, 29–30).

The Hebrew Wisdom tradition contains resources for speaking of Wisdom as an emanation of God and also for seeing Wisdom as capable of 'passing into holy souls' (Solomon 7, 27) to make them friends of God and prophets. It is not after all such a gargantuan leap from this to speaking of an eternal 'Word' of God which is capable of being enfleshed in a human being, as being 'made flesh'.

This provides a quite different perspective from that of the Synoptic Gospels, and it is the basis for a great deal of speculative development by the Church fathers. If we were to continue such development in our own context, we might reflect that the Greek word *Logos* can be translated in many ways – as 'Word', 'Speech', 'Thought', 'Intellect', 'Wisdom', or even 'Reason'. It is a strangely impersonal term, and it does not seem to refer to a self-subsistent being, or one who exists as a person, in the sense of having a distinct and unique consciousness and agency. It suggests, rather, the act or quality of a personal being. For it is persons who have wisdom or intellect or speech, as a quality of their being.

If God is regarded as a Mind, then we might think of the Word as a thought in the mind of God, or rather as that mind itself insofar as it generates intelligible thoughts. Yet this Word cannot be just one thought among many others. It is, to use a word used by John, *monogenes*, generated as one, not as many – or, as many scholars hold, simply 'unique in kind', without specific reference to generation. There are certain to be many (a potentially infinite number of) thoughts in God, and perhaps God, if God is temporal, thinks creatively and in constantly novel ways. But there is one undivided Wisdom, uniquely generated (the traditional phrase in English is 'only-begotten') by that incomprehensible 'unlimited ocean of being' from which all things are generated. The generation of Wisdom or 'the Word' is necessary and without temporal beginning. As those who opposed Arianism in the early history of Christian thought said, there never was a time when the Word was not. The Word is 'with' God, in that it is eternally generated as the content of the divine mind. The Word 'is' God, in that it is not created by a contingent divine decision, but is part of the divine being.

Although John begins with the eternal God, the Gospel is of course about Jesus, seen as the Word of God 'made flesh'. This perspective gives a different tone to the narrative. Throughout John's Gospel, Jesus speaks as one who sees and hears God clearly and intimately: 'He whom God has sent speaks the words of God' (3, 34); 'As I hear, I judge' (5, 30); 'The Son can do nothing on his own, but only what he sees the Father doing' (5, 19); 'Glorify me in your own presence with the glory that I had in your presence before the world existed' (17, 5).

The Father 'speaks' through Jesus, and Jesus 'sees' the Father. Moreover, Jesus remembers that he pre-existed with God, was sent by God, and came down from heaven, 'where he was before' (6, 62). He is 'the one who descended from heaven, the Son of Man' (3, 13).

We do not know what sort of reflection on these Johannine texts might have taken place in the communities which first accepted them as canonical. But the texts are canonical for contemporary Christians too, and as we reflect on them from our own philosophical viewpoint, we might be clear that it was not the human Jesus who existed before the world existed, for 'the Word *became* flesh' (1, 14; italics mine). The Word was not always flesh. The Johannine Jesus knows that, as unfleshed Word which has now taken flesh in him, he existed with God in glory. It follows that when Jesus says 'I' in these Johannine speeches, he does not refer only to a human subject of action and experience. He refers to an eternal spiritual reality which has, as it were, suffused or embraced (or perhaps been enfleshed in) the human subject.

For us a crucial question is this: how can a spiritual and divine reality 'become' a human, created subject? Certainly not by ceasing to be a divine reality. So the divine reality must, as most of the Church fathers said, in some sense add a human subject to itself. When the Word, the divine reality, returns to heaven from whence it came, it now has humanity, a human subject, added to it, having been particularised in a human subject.

Jesus is the Word of God 'made flesh'. Yet it is not said to be the divine Word who speaks in or through Jesus. The Word is not the speaker. 'I declare what I have seen in the Father's presence' (8, 30). In fact the impersonal nature of the expression 'the Word' is remarkable. A 'word' is spoken by a person, but is not itself a person. The one who speaks is the Father. This suggests that the Word is God's communicative and expressive thought. This thought has an eternal existence; the thought of the world exists before the world exists. A thought does not speak – it is the speech of the Father; we may say 'it does what it hears'. The thought 'becomes flesh', as the thought takes form as a human subject. Though it is the thought of God, it becomes expressed in the mind of a human being. It is as though a thought had passed from one mind to another. The thoughts of God become the thoughts of a man, insofar as they can be restricted to such a finite form. The thoughts of God take shape, or are expressed so far as is possible, in the mind of a man.

Thoughts can be enfleshed; they can 'take flesh' – as when an architect's blueprint is made real in concrete or stone. Perhaps we should not think of the Word in John as a person or a subject of experience at all. It is interesting that many other metaphors that John uses of Jesus – water, bread, light, life, and way – are also impersonal. That may tell us something important about how John thought of Jesus.

We may then, at least provisionally and no doubt partially, think of the Word as the self-expressive thought of God. This expression leads us to think not so much of Father and Son but of Thinker and Thought. Of course John speaks of Jesus as Son of God as well. That will qualify the impersonality of many of John's metaphors. Yet it seems right, theologically, to think of the eternal Word as the eternally expressed thought of God. It is the Thought which is *monogenes theos* (John 1, 18), the uniquely generated aspect of God. Then God's Thought is made real and particular in material form in Jesus. Jesus is the Ideal made physical or given finite particularity. As C. H. Dodd put it when writing about John's distinctive use of the phrase 'the Son of Man', this is 'the *alethinos anthropos* . . . or the Platonic Idea of Man' (Dodd, 1953, p. 244).

Many Patristic writers, seeking a philosophical way of putting this, took the Word to be a personal subject or *prosopon*, which was the real agent in Jesus' actions. In recent times, Kasemann has argued that this was a correct perception and that John represents Jesus as 'God striding over the earth', virtually untouched by real human grief and suffering. Generally speaking, however, in post-Enlightenment philosophy free personal agency is essential to true humanity, so if Jesus was truly human, he must have been a personal agent. Thus, in an apparent reversal of some Patristic ways of speaking, we may say that there is only one personal 'subject' in Jesus; but it is not the Word, which is not a distinct subject of consciousness and will at all. There is only the human subject in Jesus, but that subject perfectly expresses the divine Ideal or self-communicative expression of God. This reformulation is not a rejection of Patristic thinking. It is a different way of formulating the mystery of the union of eternal Word and human person in Jesus, a way which is forced by changes in general philosophical outlook to take greater account of the post-medieval emphasis on the creative autonomy of the human person and the relatively non-substantial or supra-personal character of abstract terms such 'Word' or 'Wisdom'.

Accordingly, when Jesus speaks of a return to the place from whence he came (the heart or mind of God, 'the bosom of God' – John 1, 18), we can think of this as a return of God's self-expressive creation to the divine realm, now embodied in fleshly form. Jesus is a real human subject, conformed wholly to the eternal divine Ideal. So when the Johannine Jesus says 'I', he can be taken as meaning, 'this human subject, which is the image or perfect human expression of the eternal thought of God'. This expressive thought is embodied in this man and remains united to him forever. The Word, on this model, is an eternal possibility made actual, first as an eternal Ideal in the mind of God, and then (incarnated) in a finite subject.

Most theologians have always thought that God, in the eternal being, necessarily knows all possible states, which include both good and bad. God cannot be said to love all possible states, since God does not love, desire, or approve of the bad states, even though God cannot fail to know what they are. Some good states, however – and perhaps all compossible good states that can be actualised to a supreme, or greatest possible, degree – are actualised within the being of God, and those are states that God loves and finds beatitude in loving. (We should not think of this as a temporal sequence, of course.) Then we can think of the Word, in its most extensive sense, as an eternal set of good states that God knows, wills, and loves. This set is 'with' God, as being the willed object of divine love. And it 'is' God, because these states are the essential content of the divine mind, without which God would not be as God is. This was certainly the sort of thing Anselm had in mind when he spoke of God as 'that than which no greater can be conceived'.

We are in no position to say exactly and exhaustively what God actualises in the divine mind. But we can claim to know that among the contents of the divine mind there is the ideal of human person-hood that Christians call 'the Word', the pattern of a perfected human life particularised in a specific historical context and society. It is this ideal which is embodied in the human subject, Jesus of Nazareth.

We can find here a form of Trinity, as God actualises (as 'the Father' or source of all) a supreme set of objective values ('the Son') from the set of all possible states through the life-giving power of the Spirit, who unifies all those values in one integrated experience. Theological reflection on the person of Jesus has naturally and inevitably developed and changed in many ways over the past two thousand years. It has taken John's Gospel as a primary datum for such reflection, but that Gospel has usually been interpreted with the aid of concepts and worldviews that almost certainly differ from those of the original writers of the Gospel.

It has proved very difficult to recover the thought forms of its original writers and readers. Raymond Brown has argued that the Gospel was written for a beleaguered sect that had rather Gnostic tendencies, was very inward-looking, and exhibited a great deal of hostility to outsiders and to Jews in particular (Brown, 1979). Many commentators read the Gospel as teaching that 'the brethren' are to be loved but 'the world' is to be hated, and all its inhabitants who do not accept Jesus as the emissary of God are destined to be lost. Despite these very negative comments, Raymond Brown takes John to be a positive Gospel of God's incarnation and universal love.

Wayne Meeks, also, provides an interpretation of John's Gospel which, he says, is 'diametrically opposed' to seeing Jesus as a reconciling union between spirit and the finite world (Meeks, in Ashton, 1986, p. 160). Jesus appears here as 'the Stranger par excellence', forcing a division between the world and the faithful. The faithful are an alienated and misunderstood community which makes totalistic and exclusive claims even as it splits and fades into insignificance.

It may seem odd, in view of this interpretation, that the Church later took this Gospel as a vital source of doctrine, when these commentators see it as an expression of the beliefs of a peripheral and persecuted community which was soon to die out. The point is that no Christian generation has ever rested content with the presumed intentions of its forebears, even when they (mistakenly) think that this is what they are doing. They are mistaken because there is no possible access to what the writers meant in their time and culture. Often if we do get some idea of what they meant, it is so alien to our own understanding of the world that we cannot identify with it.

A Scripture is the foundation document of a community. But Scriptures are reread and reinterpreted in many diverse communities. And it has been so from the beginning. As Gunther Bornkamm has put it, 'The first task is still to arrive at a critical understanding of the manifold varieties of early Christianity with an eye to their original intention, to take on board the questions that arise from their extremely diverse historical settings, and then to present freshly, in one's own language and according to one's own way of thinking, the gospel of Christ' (Bornkamm, in Ashton, 1986, p. 94). Bornkamm still speaks of discovering original intentions, and to that extent he is still trapped in the thought that it is possible to see what is in another person's mind and exactly what that person means. My sense, after a life spent in discussing philosophy and theology, is that we can never know exactly what is in others' minds. And in a way it does not matter; what they wrote stands on its own, whatever they think they meant.

There is, of course, a particular view of language here: that words have meaning only when they are used within communities of speakers. Those meanings are always flexible and changing, even within groups, and the ambiguities, complexities, and even the contradictions and mistakes of language are parts of the meanings it may convey. Thus we often have to think of other ways of putting things, we often look for new translations of ancient texts, and we often value new interpretations that we have not previously thought of.

Still, even if it is not possible to get into another's mind, it is possible to get a feel for what they were concerned with, what problems they tried to solve, and what their expressed interests were. And Bornkamm is right; we need to try to understand the sort of social groups, and the main values and problems of those groups, in order not to assimilate them too closely to the very different values and problems of our historical and social epoch. But then we need to present freshly, in our own language, what the texts they produced are able to say to us, given our understanding of the Christian Gospel as a whole.

For Scriptural texts are not just historical records. They are vehicles of spiritual insight and encounter. John's Gospel, in presenting Jesus as the eternal Word of the Father, offers formative and definitive material for reflection on the nature of the God who is revealed in the person of Jesus.

One basic question about the Gospel is whether it presents a totalistic and exclusive view, written only for a small elite who are to be saved from a condemned and doomed world, or whether it is a Gospel of God's universal love which is to unite all things in the divine life, so that the whole world will be saved. Raymond Brown stresses the clear elements of universalism that are present in John: Jesus takes away the sin of the *world* (John 1, 29), even though in John 'the world' stands for all that is hateful and opposed to God. Jesus draws *all men* to himself (John 12, 32) and is 'the light that lightens *everyone* who comes into the world'. Barnabas Lindars writes that 'John's own understanding of the gospel message rises above sectarianism to embrace all humanity' (Lindars, 1990, p. 58). It may have been the case that the Gospel was the work of a sect destined to die out, but the 'great church' which took over the Gospel was able to reinterpret it in a much more inclusive way – though that inclusive interpretation is still not accepted by all Christian readers of the text.

Wayne Meeks' 'Stranger' who divides the world from the spirit is not after all diametrically opposed to the reconciler of heaven and earth. In the wider context of what came to be the New Testament, division and reconciliation are two movements of one historical narrative in which God creates a world which becomes estranged, enters into it in a judgment which is paradoxically also its salvation, and reunites it to the divine life. This threefold movement establishes a Trinitarian pattern for thinking about the being of God: the one who stands apart from the world as its creator enters into it as its Saviour and remains in it in a different form to unite it to the divine as its Sanctifier.

John does not speak of God as God might be apart from any creation. But he speaks of a God who truly relates to creation in a threefold way. When God creates a cosmos from which other persons are generated, God also (by the Word) defines the ideal goals towards which it strives, and (by the Spirit) works within the universe to realise those ideals. God as Father is the origin of everything other than the necessary divine nature itself. God as Word defines an objective Ideal for created beings, though that ideal may be worked out and developed in many creative ways by finite persons. God as Spirit works synergistically and progressively to realise the Ideal, objectively existing in the mind of God; and in that development finite persons may play their creative part in giving specific form to their final goal.

This threefold division might not have arisen if it had not been for the fact that Jesus was seen as the Word of the Father, with the power to send the Spirit to his disciples (John 16, 7). The human Jesus is clearly not the creator of the universe, nor does he exist within all human hearts to unite them to the divine. Thus Word, Spirit, and Creator are separated by their different functions in relation to creation, even though it is the one God in different aspects of being who creates and who participates in creation as the foreshadowing of its ideal goal, and who unites all creation to the divine.

It is creation that makes the cooperative and creative realisation and contemplation of distinctively new values possible. God becomes one who creates finite persons, who relates in love – in compassion, respect, appreciation, and shared action and experience – to finite persons, and who unites finite persons to the divine in one communion of being. Seen thus, the Trinity expresses the nature of God as love. The threefold form of divine love – as creating finite persons, relating in love to them, and uniting them to the divine life – is the manifestation (the 'exegesis', John says in his prologue) of the supreme goodness of God as creative, self-giving, and universally inclusive love.

I have put this 'freshly in my own language', as an interpretation of John from within my own very different historical context. Yet this idea of the uniting of finite persons in God, of a final union of human and divine, is a distinctive feature of John's Gospel. The 'farewell discourses' of John (13, 31–16, 33) and Jesus' Prayer to the Father (17, 1–26) form an important basis for the development of the Patristic doctrine of *theosis*, of the uniting of humans to the being of God. The Johannine Jesus speaks about the unity of Father, Son, and believers in a series of brief but remarkable sentences: 'I am in the Father, and the Father in me' (14, 11); he prays for the disciples 'that they all may be one. As you, Father, are in me, and I am in you, may they also be in us . . . so that they may be one, as we are one, I in them, and you in me' (17, 21–23). The mutual indwelling of Father and Son, and so in some sense their identity, is here clearly asserted. But it is also affirmed that it is the ultimate destiny of the disciples to be included in this unity.

It is in these discourses that John has Jesus explicitly speak of the Spirit. Jesus says, 'I will pray the Father, and he will give you another Paraclete, to be with you for ever' (14, 16). Jesus ascends to heaven, to the presence of God, but the Spirit remains with the disciples, and indeed within them. The Spirit 'will teach you all things and remind you of all I told you' (14, 26). The Spirit will witness to Jesus, give hope of things to come, and show the disciples what the Father has shown in Jesus.

According to these descriptions, the Spirit does not speak of itself. Sent by Jesus (John 20, 22), or by the Father at the request of Jesus, it witnesses to God's revelation in Jesus, and it is in that sense that it is 'the Spirit of truth' (14, 16): 'He will take what is mine and declare it to you' (16, 14). Spirit does not here seem to be an independent personal reality who has conversations with the Father and the Son in some internal Trinitarian society. Spirit seems to be a form of continuing and strengthening divine presence in human lives which unveils and makes the God revealed in Jesus present to those who seek to follow Jesus.

It is, we may say, the Spirit who makes God present in the lives of the disciples and enables the disciples to participate in the life of God. Jesus prays that the disciples may have the same sort of union with God (they are to be 'in' God, and God is to be 'in' them) as he has with God. Jesus has direct and intimate access to the mind of God (and so is in God), and God acts freely and fully in and through Jesus (and so God is in him). So the disciples are to make such a way of being their goal, increasing in knowledge of God and in the ability to mediate the love of God. They cannot do this on their own. It is the Spirit who acts in them to help them achieve this goal, making God known to them and making the divine love active in them.

The importance of this basis for the Christian life is that God is not viewed as a remote creator or a divine dictator. God is a being of supreme beauty and goodness in whose life we are invited to participate. And God acts in and through us, so that human lives are intended to be a growth into conscious, continuing, and inseparable communion with perfect Beauty. This is life in God, produced and sustained by the Father, patterned on the Son, and empowered by the Spirit.

I am not, of course, suggesting that this is the one correct interpretation of John's Gospel. On the contrary, I am insisting that there is no such thing as one correct interpretation and that, moreover, interpretations must change with more general frameworks of ideas which bring to the fore different aspects of a very complex and many-stranded text. One can see in John's Gospel, I suggest, the basis for a developed view, such as the one here, of the eternal Word or thought of God fully and without constraint manifested in and through the life of a man, Jesus. One can see the Spirit as the power of God which gives the divine thought actuality, life, and vivacity and creativity. In God there is the thinker, the intelligible thought, and the creative power of being, which realises the eternal thought, first in the divine being itself; then in the emergence of finite persons within an intelligible physical universe; then in the dynamic and temporal human life of Jesus, which reconciles an estranged creation to its creator; and finally in progress towards a loving communion of persons with each other and with God. Insofar as this captures something of the Johannine model, there is here an intelligible and spiritually profound Trinitarian description of the divine life.

CHAPTER 9

The Trinity in the Epistles

The depiction of God as threefold is clearly to be found in many of the Letters included in the New Testament. Much of this literature is earlier than the Gospels, and so it expresses thoughts that were current in some of the earliest strands of Christian belief, and probably taken for granted in the Gospels. One strand that is very clear in Paul's Letters, and not explicitly emphasised in the same way in the Gospels, is the vital importance of the experience of the Spirit in the Church. The Gospels on the whole concentrate on the life and teachings of Jesus, though of course they do so in the light of a belief in the resurrection. The passion of Jesus is of supreme importance in the Gospels, but not much is said about its atoning significance in the lives of believers.

In considering Paul's views, I shall take the Letters to the Galatians, Romans, and Corinthians as largely if not wholly written by Paul. What is most significant about them is their very strong emphasis on the presence and work of the Holy Spirit as a transforming power in the lives of believers: 'If we live by the Spirit, let us also be guided by the Spirit' (Galatians 5, 25). For Paul, Christian faith begins with a personal experience of the Spirit as a power that liberates from 'the Law'. Whereas traditionally Jews have lived by obedience to Torah, the Law, now disciples of Jesus must live by 'the law of the Spirit of life', which 'in Christ Jesus has set you free from the law of sin and of death' (Romans 8, 2). Paul even lists the virtues, the 'fruit', which the Spirit produces: 'love, joy, peace, patience, kindness, generosity, faithfulness, gentleness, and self-control' (Galatians 5, 22–23). In this sense Paul's Gospel is experiential, founded on a new experience of liberation from rules and freedom to enjoy a new quality of life.

This new experience, however, is for Paul essentially connected with the person of Jesus, and in particular with Jesus' death and resurrection. 'A person is justified not by the works of the Law but through faith in Jesus Christ' (Galatians 2, 16). To have faith in Jesus Christ is more than to assent to the proposition that Jesus was the Messiah; it is to put one's trust wholly in Jesus, to live '*en Christo*', in union with Christ. 'As many of you as were baptized into Christ have clothed yourselves with Christ' (Galatians 3, 27). What matters is to 'be baptized into Christ', to participate in the life of Christ. 'If we have died with Christ, we believe that we will also live with him' (Romans 6, 8). This again is a matter of personal experience, of dying to sin and living to God. But that experience has an ineliminable cognitive dimension. It is in union with Christ that we die to sin and in union with Christ that we rise to new life. There is an objective personal reality, the living Christ, and that Christ died on the cross, becoming 'a curse for us' (Galatians 3, 13) so that we might be liberated from evil.

Thus 'all of us, with unveiled faces, seeing the glory of the Lord as though reflected in a mirror, are being transformed into the same image from one degree of glory to another' (2 Corinthians 3, 18). Jesus, though he lived and died as a man, is now raised to glory and is unveiled as the 'visible image' of the invisible God and the ideal human person, whom we may all aspire to emulate and in whose likeness we may aspire to grow. Paul may not have a clear doctrine of divine incarnation in Jesus, but his Jesus has a cosmic dimension. There is no other human being 'in whom' we may all desire to live, and there is no merely human being in whom we could all possibly live. Paul sees Jesus as Son of God and Lord and so has a triadic image of God. This viewpoint comes out clearly in such texts as 'God has sent the Spirit of his Son into our hearts' (Galatians 4, 6). Here, God, Son, and Spirit are aspects of the divine which are known in the new experience of life in Christ. The materials for developing a doctrine of the Trinity lie ready to hand.

The cosmic dimension of Christ, according to which Christ is a cosmic reality 'in whom' all can participate, is developed further in other Letters, especially at the beginning of the Letters to the Hebrews, Ephesians, and Colossians. These Letters are widely thought to be later than the Pauline corpus, perhaps even third generation, but I think they are natural developments of the 'en Christo' theme rather than conflicts with Paul's central ideas. The 'Letter to the Hebrews', for instance, begins with a blunt statement that 'the Son' is the one 'through whom' God made the universe, who upholds the universe by his power, and who is 'the heir of all things' (Hebrews 1, 2, and 3). This is no mere human, and yet it seems other than God. Why should God make the universe 'through' another being when God is omnipotent? The impression could be given that God relates to the cosmos through an intermediary. Yet this intermediary is addressed as God (1, 8) and is said to create the cosmos himself (1, 10).

A clue to the way language is being used here may be found in Proverbs chapter 8, wherein Lady Wisdom is portrayed as the 'first-born of creation' and as rejoicing with God in the created world. It is not possible to think that Wisdom was the first creature of God, literally, since God created all things with wisdom, which God possessed before creation. So this is a personification of a divine attribute, spoken of as though it was a person. The attributes or qualities of God can therefore be spoken of as personal beings but are in reality aspects of one divine reality, which in itself is beyond all personhood. We might say, as Philo did, that as the infinity of the divine turns towards thinking of a cosmos, it takes form as Wisdom or Intellect, but that form is and remains a particular form of the divine. Or to use another metaphor, as John's Gospel puts it, the *Logos* was 'with' God and yet 'was' God.

Using terminology that belongs more to my own culture, I would say that 'the Son' (also called 'the Word') is an aspect of the divine as it conceives and relates to a specific cosmos. It is not the whole of divinity, but it is one of the forms of divinity as humans are able to conceive it. Infinite Being turns in thought towards a cosmos, taking form as Wisdom. It creates the cosmos 'through' that Wisdom – not another person, but a personalised aspect of the divine.

It is this Wisdom that 'takes human flesh' and is then known as a human person who is the '*charakter tes hypostaseos*' of God (Hebrews 1, 3) – that is, the human manifestation or 'character' of the reality of God. Far from being a person completely distinct from God, Jesus is the personal and human manifestation of God, insofar as God is the intelligible wisdom upon which our cosmos is founded. If this is true, Jesus would not have known God as an 'other' person. He would have known God as the ultimate source and sustenance of the cosmos, and in particular of the ideal unity of creature and creator, a unity that he expressed paradigmatically in his own being. God is the infinitely greater reality from which the pattern (the Word) of the cosmos is generated, a pattern which Jesus expresses in human form. It is because of this that the Johannine Jesus can regard God as 'greater than' him (John 14, 28) and yet can claim identity with God, as the expression of the communicative and creative Word of God. The thinker is in a way greater than the thought, yet the thought expresses (as fully as is possible in this medium) what the thinker is.

Jesus manifests the ideal form of a perfected human life, fulfilled by conscious unity with the Spirit of God. But Jesus is more than that. He is 'the heir of all things' and so has a destiny and a reality much greater than his human form considered alone allows. No merely human being can be the heir, the ruler and disposer, of thousands of millions of galaxies. It is in his reality as eternal Word that Jesus sustains and will finally be sovereign over the whole cosmos. The human person of Jesus will forever remain the human expression of this Word, but, although a completely authentic expression, it will far from exhaust the full reality of the Word. The archetypal pattern of the cosmos will find its completion in the fully realised embodiment of the divine pattern in a communion of persons interpenetrated and transfigured by the divine Spirit. This will be the 'body of Christ' (1 Corinthians 12, 27), the cosmic Christ, a communion of personal being of which Jesus was the human forerunner on this planet. The human but transfigured human form of Jesus will always remain the authentic manifestation of the eternal Word for humanity. But what that Word will be in its totality, and in relation to all the forms of personal life the universe may contain, is far beyond anything we can now imagine.

The view of Christ as cosmic archetype and wisdom is stated clearly in the Letters to the Ephesians and Colossians. The Letter to the Ephesians says that God has 'made known to us the mystery of his will', which is 'a plan for the fullness of time, to gather up all things in him [Christ], things in heaven and things on earth' (1, 10). All things (*panta*) in the whole created universe, not just on the planet earth, are to be united in Christ. We know that the universe is much bigger than could have been imagined by the writers of the New Testament, but the point is clear: every created thing is to be united in Christ, the eternal Wisdom and Word of God. The completion of God's plan for creation will be when the divine archetypal plan is fleshed out or embodied in a perfected universe, when all creation will be united to God.

And Colossians affirms that 'Christ is the image of the invisible God', that 'all things have been created through him and for him', and that 'through him God was pleased to reconcile to himself all things, whether on earth or in heaven' (1, 15–20). This Christ is not just a human person; it is divine wisdom itself, which was embodied on earth in a human person. And that wisdom is destined to include all things in itself, liberated from evil and transformed by the Spirit. At that time, at the end of history, all beings will be full and authentic images and expressions of the divine, the reality of which is infinite. We will be 'the body of Christ' (Colossians 1, 18), as we already are in embryo, the body of divine Wisdom, manifesting the endless beauty of that divine stream of creative thought which will work through us, express itself in us, and be known fully by us – though each of us alone, and even all of us together, will only be a minute part of its glory.

This does not entail that we will be passive expressions of a solely divine intention. We may contribute to the specific realised forms of the divine plan, filling it out with our own minute yet truly creative intentions and acts. Thus the Spirit will work in us and with us as we fill out the forms of the cosmic Christ in an endless creative communion of persons who are parts of a vast throng of created species and forms of life.

The divine life will then not be just a 'Trinity of persons'. It will be a vast multitude of persons, created, sustained, and fulfilled by the one divine and unlimited being who generates them, makes itself known to them in forms like theirs, liberates them from all that leads them away from their primal source, and guides them by an inward spiritual power towards the goal of a truly cosmic communion of love in which self-abandonment and self-realisation have become one.

The New Testament, taken as a whole, thus speaks of God as a dynamic, creative, and relational reality, a reality known in a basic threefold relation to a created world. God envisages the world, takes form within it, and unites it progressively and synergistically – by cooperative and creative action – to the divine life. There is a real unfolding story of the Trinity, and it is in the unfolding of that history that God is Trinity. That seems to be a very natural implication of both the Gospels and the Epistles. They, of course, only exist because they contain a record of and reflections upon the deeds and words, the death, and the resurrection of Jesus and because they witness to him as the risen Lord. It is therefore a necessary part of a consideration of the Trinity to make some attempt, however inadequate, at understanding what can be meant by this and to see what can be meant by identifying humanity and divinity in the person of Jesus.

CHAPTER 10

The Idea of Incarnation

Jesus is presented in the Gospels as a man who is uniquely close to – so close as to be in some sense identical with – God. So we might ask, how close can a human be to God? Jacob Neusner tells of how in ancient Judaism outstanding rabbis were sometimes said to be 'embodiments of Torah'. They lived in such obedience to the law of God that they seemed to embody it in themselves. It does seem possible for a person to have such an intimate knowledge of God that they could be said to share in the knowledge of God (obviously in a way and to a degree possible for human minds). It is possible for them to have such love for God that they might feel no separation between themselves and God but rather a unity of heart and mind; many mystics speak in such a way. And it is possible for them to be so completely obedient to God that they could be said to become channels of divine action, justice, and compassion in the world. So there could exist a human being who shares in the knowledge of God, is united in love to God, and is a channel of God's love for the world. It is possible that it is God's intended destiny for every human being that they should be in such an intimate relationship with God, and perhaps that is what Paradise is.

Some might feel that this still falls short of that actual identity with God or with the Word of God that is characteristic of the Christian faith of the Church fathers. Was Jesus not the very Word of God incarnate? It is true that this is a 'Christology from below'

73

and lies in a modern tradition influenced by theologians such as Donald Baillie, sometimes called 'Spirit Christology'. Yet the Council of Chalcedon clearly stated that Jesus was 'truly man', and the fathers came to affirm that Jesus had a truly human will and was not just God in the outward form of a human person. They also typically asserted that the exact form of identity between the human will and the divine Word was unique and wrapped in ineffable mystery.

Modern thought stresses the freedom and autonomy of human persons more emphatically than did the thought of classical antiquity, and this will make a difference to the way divine-human identity is interpreted. It will make sense to start with a strong affirmation of the full humanity of Jesus and then ask in what way this humanity could be identified with the divine. It will make sense to say that Jesus is a fully human person, and not just an impersonal 'human nature' possessed by a divine person. But it will also be possible to affirm the absolute ontological uniqueness of Jesus among all human persons. Jesus may be unique in being fully united to God from the first moment of his earthly existence and in living by the full and unimpeded power of the Spirit. Only by a unique divine initiative could this be possible, and it must be distinguished from the idea of a man who simply shows love and wisdom in a spectacular way by his own power. The absolute moral purity and inspired wisdom of Jesus is realised by specific divine action, which makes the human subject an unimpeded medium of divine love and divine action. It must do so without frustrating the true humanity of Jesus, who, as 'Son of Man', is a foreshadowing of the destiny of all humans, the eternal ideal made present by a unique act of divine power in time.

Human beings in general are persons who have their own centres of creatively free action – that is an important part of the definition of a 'person'. God may seek to persuade and guide them, and draw them to the divine self. But they will remain masters of their own destiny to a large extent. It is possible, and Christians believe it has happened, that finite persons should fall away from God and become isolated and self-destructive beings trapped in hatred, greed, and ignorance. But it is also possible – and it is God's desire – that they should increase in love for God and for creation. This happens by 'repentance' (*metanoia*, turning from self to God) and 'faith' (complete trust in God's guidance and God's promises). For virtually all human beings, earthly life is a journey from alienation towards unity with the divine being.

Suppose, however, that there is a person not born in such alienation, a person whose will is turned to God in love and trust from the first. This would be a person who was never egoistic or overwhelmed by self-centred passion; who was always mindful and self-controlled, compassionate and loving; and who experienced a constant sense of the presence of God and the power of the Spirit prompting and inspiring their thoughts and feelings. Such a person would not need repentance or faith in the sense of contrition for wrongdoing and commitment to a God who is not fully known and felt. That person could only exist by an extraordinary and specific act of God, exercised continuously throughout a whole human life, to preserve the person from evil and fill a whole life with the spirit of wisdom and love. Is such a person possible? The conception is not self-contradictory. It is theoretically possible.

In many Indian religious traditions it is the idea of a 'liberated soul', or one, such as Gautama Buddha perhaps, who has achieved Enlightenment. A liberated soul has passed beyond the sense of ego, has achieved wisdom (omniscience in respect of all things leading to liberation, in one Buddhist formula) and compassion for all beings, and has entered into Nirvana – or (in one formulation) into a state of perfect selflessness and bliss or (in some Hindu traditions) oneness with the Self of All. In those traditions, there is not always talk of grace, as the perfected life is said to be attained through disciplined training over many reincarnations, and there is often no personal creator God who could create such a perfected soul.

There is an analogy within Christianity, however. For after death, in 'eternal life', Christians hope for a way of existence that is indissoluble from love of God, that is beyond the possibility of falling back into evil, and that is grounded in beatitude – happiness in the contemplation of perfect Beauty and Love.

Thus a perfected life, a life beyond evil and grounded in perfect love, is not only possible, but it is a positive hope for many religious believers. Might it not seem appropriate, then, that a creator God whose purpose for humanity is that it should achieve such a goal should provide, by a special and unique act of divine power, an example of a perfected life in human history, as a sign of the promise and reality of its final destiny?

The idea is not that God 'turns into' a human being, or that God completely controls the thoughts and deeds of a human being. Such an idea would conflict with the belief codified at the Council of Chalcedon that Jesus is fully human in every respect except for sin. In the case of all human beings, God has complete knowledge of all they feel and think. But the feelings and thoughts of most human beings often conflict with the will of God, and so God must preserve a certain distance from them. God knows what the feelings are, and in a sense this means that God feels them. But God does not identify with them, and no one can say that these are God's own feelings or feelings in accord with God's own nature.

In the case of a grace-perfected life, however, there would be no alienating distance between God's nature and this human nature. One could rightly say that the acts of this human person accord perfectly with what God wills and with what God is. And the likeness is not accidental. It is essential, for it is prompted and guided by God.

Would this take away true human freedom? If it is essential to human nature that humans should be creatively free, it cannot be the case that God 'runs' a human person, like a puppeteer making a puppet do exactly what he wants it to do. This question is like the question Could we be creatively free in Paradise? to which the response must be that we will be freer in Paradise than on earth, because we will not be hampered by uncontrolled desires and destructive feelings such as resentment and vindictiveness. We will have our own creative decisions to make, and they will not conflict with the will of God – for God's will is precisely that we should be both creative and oriented to intrinsically worthwhile values, which we may freely imagine and originate. God will increase our free creativity, not obliterate it.

A crucial idea here is that of divine-human synergy. This is a term which occurs just once in the New Testament (2 Corinthians 6, 1), and it means 'working together'. When two people work together, the creativity of each can be enhanced. They may spark off ideas as they collaborate, and each may contribute something of value that neither could have done on their own. God is not, of course, another finite person. But God is personal, and God and finite persons can cooperate, and in the process both may be changed. Finite persons may be changed by having their imaginations and capacities enhanced. God may be changed by coming to know as actual certain values that otherwise would not have existed and by contributing to the knowledge and ability of creative persons.

It is not that God has just one preordained plan which finite persons have to work out in a predetermined and precise way. God's plan is that persons should cooperatively work together to create new forms of goodness. It is the working out, the synergy, that creates new values. This gives an even more important role for finite persons. They can contribute positively to the cosmic creative process, and perhaps the cooperative creation and contemplation of ever-new values is a very great form of goodness that only a God who synergistically interacts with finite persons could bring about.

A grace-perfected human life would be creatively free and yet incapable of falling into evil. It could be created by God as an objective realisation of the ideal goal of human persons. As such, it could appropriately be seen as a realisation in history of the ideal goal in the mind of God, enacted in and through a living human person 'who in every respect has been tested as we are, yet without sin' (Hebrews 4, 15). It would be a human life, truly a subject of human thought, experience, and action, which could be identified with God, or with the intention in the mind of God that forms the pattern and goal of the creation of this planet.

On this view, Jesus is a truly human person, but he is not only a human person. He is also, by what I have called a synergistic union, the earthly manifestation of God. There is the deepest possible unity, original and indissoluble, between his humanity and the mind and will of God. In that sense, Jesus is God. But he is not God *simpliciter*. He is God insofar as God turns towards the world in compassion and takes form within the world – God as participant in the world. Thus when Jesus prays to the Father, it is the human person, limited in power and knowledge, one finite being among others, wholly dependent upon the creator for his existence and nature, who voices his human desires and intentions, and attests his total dependence upon the transcendent creator of all. It is not God as the eternal Word who prays to God as Father – which would be a case of the divine speaking to itself. It is the human person of Jesus, who is truly in some sense identical with God as participant, who prays to God as creator. We might say that one aspect of the earthly manifestation of God prays to the cosmic reality of God as infinite creator.

At first sight, this may not seem to make sense. But consider the case of those recent philosophers who claim that mental states are identical with brain states. It does not follow that everything you can say about mental states can be said about brain states. For instance, I may have a mental image that has internal spatial relations and colours, and it may be said to be identical with some brain state. But my brain state does not have or contain the same sort of internal spatial relations and colours. We could say, however, that 'whatever it is' that mental states and brain states are different aspects of has the properties of both sensations of colour and electrochemical discharges. For a double-aspect identity theorist (such as John Searle and also, as it happens, me), there is just one reality with a complex set of properties, but those properties can be sorted into their two different aspects. Then we can say that a human person consists of both mental and brain states, inseparably connected, it seems, at least under the conditions of existence within this universe.

In an analogous way, we could say that the human Jesus is identical with God in the following way: 'whatever it is' that unites both divine and human natures in Jesus forms one unitary reality, but within that unity two separate aspects can be distinguished – the finite and human, and the infinite and divine. The divine aspect is the eternal turning of the divine to take form in the created order, and the human aspect is the synergistic dependence of the human upon that divine aspect. The human Jesus does not pray to his own divine aspect, but rather to the divine in its mode of being the creator and sustainer of all. We could say that the divine-human unity prays to the Father, as long as we are careful to add, 'in the human aspect of that unity'. God, in his manifestation as the one turned towards the world to take form as a particular participant, and in the finite aspect of that manifestation, prays to God, in his manifestation as the transcendent creator of all.

These words, 'manifestation' and 'aspect', are hardly fully satisfactory. They are, perhaps, not much better than the traditional formulation 'God, in the person of the Son, and in the human nature of that person, prays to God in the person of the Father'. 'Manifestation', it could be said, merely translates 'person', and 'aspect' translates 'nature'.

If the translation has any advantage, it lies mainly in the fact that 'person' in its modern sense can mislead people, and has misled some theologians, into thinking that there are three distinct minds and wills in God which converse with one another. And the word 'nature' can mislead people into thinking that the humanity of Jesus is somehow impersonal, not a creative subject of action and experience but instead an abstract nature whose subject (*hypostasis*) is only God, or perhaps God the Son.

Both these views are, I think, incorrect. By contrast, I wish to emphasise that there is only one mind and will in God (that is essential, in my view, to believing in one God) and that Jesus is a real human creative subject of action, whose unity with God is synergistic or one of total cooperation (that is essential, in my view, to believing that Jesus is fully human).

In Jesus there is a real and unique unity of the divine mind and a human mind, but that should not be conceived as the mind (or 'person') of the eternal Word subsuming, or taking over, the human mind. On this interpretation, the Word is not a 'mind' in the relevant sense of a distinct and separate subject of creative action and unique experience. Between the uncreated mind of the threefold God and the finite mind of Jesus there is in one way a complete ontological disparity, a difference of kind. They do not compete for the same ontological space, as the personalities of human schizophrenics may. In Jesus there is a compound unity of a human subject who expresses the eternal thought of God and the divine subject who exists in three forms of being and who wills Jesus' life and thought to express the eternal Word.

Jesus is called 'son of God', and thus 'begotten by' God, for he is the one anointed to liberate humanity from evil. Just as 'son' is a metaphor (meaning, roughly, chosen by God), so 'begotten' is a metaphor meaning 'manifesting in human terms what God is'. The creator is called 'Father' because that is what Jesus called the divine. The Spirit is 'the spirit of Jesus', because the Spirit can make personal encounter with God through Jesus present in all ages and places.

In this way we can see that 'begetting' is not a form of creating and that thinking of the Father as bringing about or choosing to actualise a Son, however eternally and non-temporally, can be very misleading. Rather, God chooses Jesus to manifest what God eternally is, by the power of the Spirit. This is a specific activity of God, but not one of 'creating a separate Son'. The Word of God is the eternal ideal in the mind of God which Jesus will actualise on earth. The Spirit is the creative energy of God which empowers and fills the inner life of Jesus.

Does this make Jesus divine? It does not confer omnipotence and omniscience. But it makes Jesus not only the realisation of the divine ideal, but also the one through whom God acts decisively to liberate the world from the bondage of evil. Jesus, Christians believe, is by the power of the Spirit both the revelation of the goal of union with God and the one who establishes the definitive Way to such union. Jesus is uniquely both God-with-us and the Saviour of the world. That is what the Patristic writers wanted to assert. But the terminology they developed, partly from Greek philosophical sources, failed to affirm the full and creatively free humanity of Jesus and the full participation of a passionate God in the human world. What I have tried to do here is provide a conceptual framework which will more clearly preserve those affirmations of faith.

PART III

The Trinity, Immanent and Economic

CHAPTER 11

Why Three?

Christianity is founded on belief in the divinity of Jesus, and also on belief in the transcendence over all finite things of the creator God. Difficult though it was in the context of Jewish monotheism to think of God as having two distinct forms of divinity in this way, it seems an inevitable consequence of Christian belief. But Christians believe in a *threefold* God, and it has not always seemed clear, even to Christian theologians, that this was an obvious implication of Christian faith. At least one major Christian theologian of recent times has questioned whether belief in a threefold God is strictly necessary for Christians.

In an important paper, 'Why Three?' (Wiles, 1967), the theologian and Patristics scholar Maurice Wiles shows that Christian writers in the first few Christian centuries were quite unclear and diverse in their allocation of roles to the three persons of the Trinity – although he admits that the Trinitarian formula as used in liturgy was present from the earliest times. Among the things that were unclear were these: whether the Spirit was a different person from the Son, whether Son or Spirit could more properly be termed the 'Wisdom' and the 'Love' of God, and whether the activities of the persons in relation to created reality were indivisible or indistinguishable.

After recounting some main differences of view between major writers of those early years, he proposes that the idea of divine threefoldness is 'an arbitrary analysis of the activity of God, which though of value in Christian thought and devotion is not of essential significance' (Wiles, 1957, p. 15). I think the word 'arbitrary' is too strong, although it is true that the activities of God could easily be described in different ways.

For example, if you think of what might be said to make the idea of a mind-like, purposive, and supremely valuable creator of the cosmos intelligible, you could say that such a creator would have to know all possible states it could create, evaluate them and perhaps actualise some of them in the divine being itself, appreciate them when actualised, and maybe create new sorts of possible states which might arise from what had already been created. It might create other personal beings to whom it might relate, might cooperate with created persons, might guide and inspire them, might accept their experiences into the divine experience, might act to liberate them from the estrangement into which some of them might fall, and might enable them to share in the divine life, forming a communion of love between creator and creatures. As it happens, I think God actually does all these things.

There are many different sorts of divine activity here – perhaps ten or eleven. From this list, would you come to choose just three as the 'true' forms of divine activity? And would you call these 'persons' or even 'modes of being' in any meaningful sense? Actually it would not be absurd to do so, even though other ways of dividing God up would remain possible. It would not be absurd, because if you are looking for a Christian description of God, it might be guided by the key teaching that 'God is love'. For divine love to be possible in the way that we experience it in our world, God, it seems, would have to create other personal beings, would have to know what they were, and would have to delight in their existence and care for them – love could require no less. So will (creative power), knowledge, and love (as a conscious relationship of appreciation and delight, and of compassion and companionship) would be essential to a loving creator of a world such as this one.

These divisions are reminiscent of the Augustinian triad of memory, understanding, and will. They are slightly different, and Augustine himself used different categorisations in different places, so they should not be regarded as definitive and uniquely apposite. The lesson is that speculation does not give one definitive threefold characterisation of God, although it is plausible to arrive at a basic threefold division of some sort. It would not be just arbitrary to say that a creative cosmic mind would have some form of understanding, intentionality, and affectivity.

It is not insignificant that a threefold analysis of the Creator is a rather natural one, even though not wholly definitive. This analysis is fleshed out much more if we consider further what it is for God to create, know, and love societies of other persons, in the light of some specific assertions of Christian revelation. Most important is the basic Christian claim that Jesus, as a fully human person, makes the Creator fully present and active in a human life. This forces a real distinction in God between God as transcendent creator, the knower of all possible realities, and God as somehow embodied in a human life. It forces at least a binitarian doctrine of God, as both Wiles and James Mackey have suggested. Christians need God transcendent and God incarnate. But why have a third element, the Spirit? Augustine's suggestion that the Spirit is 'love' makes it an impersonal bond between two persons and thus, radically unlike Father and Son, hardly a distinct mode of being at all. Moreover, the view that came to be commonly accepted that the external acts of the Trinity are indivisible seems to make the separate existence of a Spirit unnecessary in any case – thus Wiles' hesitation about having a Trinitarian doctrine.

When you examine Christian experience in worship, however, the Spirit can be seen as absolutely necessary if a connection is to be made between contemporary people and Jesus, the incarnate God. In fact you might even be tempted to say that it is Jesus who is unnecessary, not the Spirit. For there needs to be some contact between the transcendent God and human lives, which are destined for union with God. This contact will be an immanent power that can transform human lives, and it will be the power of God. As Sarah Coakley puts it, Spirit is the power which 'incorporates the created realm into the life of God' (Coakley, 1993, p. 36). Spirit can be experienced as a synergistic or cooperative power that unites human lives (and maybe in some appropriate way the whole creation) within 'that divine and perfected creation' which is the being (the 'body') of the glorified Son (Coakley, 1993, p. 38).

Despite this temptation, Jesus cannot in fact be eliminated because the Spirit is precisely the Spirit of the Eternal Word, whose incarnate life defines the character the Spirit brings about in Jesus' disciples and expresses the fulfilment and consummation of the divine purpose for creation. There is an overwhelming reason for a Triune God in the Christian experience of worshipping the Creator of all, seeing the definitive ideal of divine-human union manifested in Jesus, and being transformed into that ideal by the inward power of the Spirit. There is nothing arbitrary about this.

John's Gospel refers to Jesus as the eternal Word of God, and that certainly suggests thought in the mind of an eternal God, apart from all creation. But though the Word is eternal, it relates to creation as its possibility. As it is natural for thoughts to become embodied – as when words formed in the mind come to be written on paper – so it is natural for God's thought of a human nature fulfilled and united in the divine to become embodied in flesh.

Images of the Spirit as intercessor or advocate, as one who leads to truth and one who imparts virtues to human beings, locate the Spirit within human lives as divine cooperator or helper. In the Hebrew Bible, the Spirit is identified as the 'breath' of God, giving life, inspiring, and unveiling spiritual truth. Thus we have the idea of God's thought of created being (entailing divine knowledge); God's embodiment of that thought in the created order (entailing divine will); and God's dynamic, inward, and synergistic cooperation with created being so as to unite it with the divine (entailing divine love).

As Wiles says, there is a 'need for caution in the making of dogmatic statements about the inner life of God' (Wiles, 1957, p. 17). But I think, nevertheless, that it is not just an arbitrary set of decisions that led Christians to speak of three 'persons' in God. The personal experience of Christians in the community of the Church and the witness of Scripture, slightly indefinite and diverse though it may be, lead almost inevitably towards the idea of one threefold God.

In the light of all these considerations, it is reasonable for Christians to think that the being of God, as revealed in and through Jesus, possesses a threefold structure, that God has three coexisting forms of being and action in relation to creation. This structure articulates a distinctive view of human history and existence as a process of dependence upon, alienation from, redemption by, and union with a supreme spiritual reality.

In modern English, the assertion that God is 'three persons in one substance', which is used for the Trinity in the great Christian creeds, does not convey this very well. The word 'substance' makes God seem too static, and the word 'person' is too liable to convey the idea of three distinct minds and wills. Both Karl Barth and Karl Rahner, leading theologians of Reformed and Roman Catholic

Christianity respectively, have suggested that it might be better to speak of one divine Subject, one centre of consciousness, knowledge, and will in God, which has three modes of being (*Seinsweisen*: Barth) or three modes of subsistence (*Subsistenzweisen*: Rahner), so that the one divine Lord has three different ways of possessing and manifesting Subjectivity. The expression 'mode of being' derives ultimately from the Cappadocian phrase *tropos hyparxeos*, but its use for the 'persons' of the Trinity is quite new. Nevertheless, I think it conveys quite well the thought that one thing (for instance, a butterfly) can exist in different forms (as caterpillar and butterfly) – though I am certainly not suggesting that a butterfly is an adequate analogy of the Trinity.

The mode of being that sustains the whole universe in existence is different from the mode of being that identifies itself with and acts in and through one (human) part of the universe, and it is different again from the mode of being that cooperates inwardly with all created intelligent agents to shape them into one all-inclusive communion of being. Yet these are all distinctive activities of the one supreme mind and will of God, expressed in different ways. God is one cosmic Subject, expressed in three distinct but indivisible and inseparable modes of being.

It is well known that the word 'person' – in Greek *prosopon* and in Latin *persona* – was taken from the term for the role that an actor played in a drama, or for the mask that represented that role. Theologians have been anxious to avoid the implication that God might put on or take off the roles of Father, Son, and Spirit at will, as one might take on or put off a mask. The councils of the Church have insisted that God was not first Father, then (at the Incarnation) Son, and then (after Pentecost) Spirit. That was a view they meant to exclude in regarding 'modalism' as a heresy. All three roles are essential to the being of God, and are taken by God simultaneously, as God relates to created beings. There is always in the mind of God the possibility of the will to create, to contemplate the objects of creation, to take form within creation as a realised ideal of finite being, and to integrate those objects in one divine experience, uniting creation in communion with the divine.

In saying this, we need to remember that the Father that we know as Christians is the Father of Jesus, the Son we know is known in and through the person of Jesus, and the Spirit we know is the Spirit of Jesus believed to be working within us. So what Christians claim to know of God as Trinity is dependent upon a divine revelation in the person of Jesus and depends upon the actuality of that person in human history. God may be more than this, but this is what as disciples of Jesus we can claim to know of God, and what we are entitled to claim with confidence is that God cannot be other than one who genuinely reveals himself in this way. That is, we know the Trinity as it relates to us in our history, in our universe, and in our creation; if we presume to speak of God beyond that revelation, we should be clear that we are speaking only of what seems to be presupposed by the truth of that revelation. We have no independent access to the innermost being of God.

CHAPTER 12

The Trinity and Revelation

It would be absurd to write a book on modern discussions of the Trinity without referring to the writings of Karl Barth. He has been largely responsible for a revived interest in the doctrine of the Trinity in recent theology. He is one of the chief defenders of a one-consciousness or non-social view of the Trinity – though, as I shall argue, his defence is in the end rather ambiguous. As I have mentioned, he saw that the word 'person' can be misleading for modern readers and proposed the phrase 'mode of being' for what were traditionally called the three 'persons' in God. He also made the idea of the Trinity central for Christian faith in a new way by arguing that the very idea of Christian revelation depends on the concept of the Trinity. Thus we cannot, he thought, first develop a concept of revelation and only later develop a doctrine of the Trinity. What we think Christian revelation is already implies the centrality of the Trinity for Christian faith.

In the *Church Dogmatics* (1, 1), Barth argues that the very idea of revelation – he means 'Christian revelation' – already implies a threefoldness. There is the revealer, the one who reveals; there is the act of revealing; and there is the reception of the revelation by a person – what Barth calls 'revealedness' – without which no revelation would have occurred. All three, he thinks, are in some sense identical. I believe he is right in this, though he seems to draw some implications from it which are not well founded and which could be positively misleading.

There are, of course, many alleged religious revelations in the world, of which Christianity is only one. All would agree, I think, that there needs to be a revealer, and most would agree that this is God. There has to be an 'act of revealing', but at this point many divergences arise. The act of revealing may, as in most Islamic interpretations, be performed by an angel and consist of the recitation of words which a prophet remembers or writes. In orthodox Hindu traditions, too, revelation primarily consists in the words of the Veda and Upanishads, held to have been virtually dictated, or at least inspired by, a god to seers. The 'act of revealing' is thus the verbal inspiration of prophets of seers. It is one kind of divine act, but it is rarely held to disclose the actual being or inner nature of the revealer. It usually consists in truths about the human situation or about God's commands or purposes or general nature. Such truths are propositions uttered by God, but it would not be acceptable to say that they are identical with, or are parts of, God. As one rabbinical saying puts it, 'Revelation shows what God commands, but not what God is'.

Barth thinks of Christian revelation differently. In Christian revelation, he thinks, God 'reveals *Himself*' and encounters humans as a Thou, as a personal and commanding presence. Thus Barth writes, 'God's own direct speech . . . is therefore not to be distinguished from the act of speaking, and therefore is not to be distinguished from God himself' (Barth, 1936, p. 304).

From a point of view of logic, these 'therefores' are misleading. When someone speaks, the content of what they say has to be distinguished from the linguistic and grammatical forms they use. The same content can be expressed in different languages. Perhaps translations never quite convey exactly the same thing as their originals, but there can be better and worse translations. When Christians read the Bible in translation, as most do, they think that they are getting the same message as in the original, even if it might be good to look at a number of translations to get a better idea of that message. Even if modern Christians read the original Hebrew of the Old Testament, they might get an impression very different from that conveyed to an ancient Hebrew. So it is understandable that Muslims will not allow translations of the Qur'an to be used in worship. But it is unduly optimistic to think that Muslim congregations will understand the original message of the Qur'an much better if they recite it in Arabic. There is a problem about 'getting exactly the same message'. But it does not deter most of us from thinking that we can get some understanding of what Jesus said in Aramaic, even if we read it in modern English.

So what is 'the act of speaking' in the case of Biblical revelation? Is it what God originally said, in Hebrew or Aramaic or Greek, to a prophet or evangelist? Or is it a teaching which can be translated well enough into some modern language? Or is it, perhaps, what God says directly to us as we read a translation of an ancient Biblical text? Whatever it is, in no case is it literally true that the act of speaking is identical with the speaker. Such an act is one of the things a speaker might do. It might or might not tell us something about the speaker if we infer from the speech something about the speaker's character or intentions.

Barth seems to be working with another model altogether – and it is a specifically Christian one, indeed a specifically Protestant, post-Hegelian, personalist one. Revelation is an 'event', an encounter in which one person unveils himself or herself to another, whether in literal words or not. In this sense of personal encounter, you may meet a person and yet be almost totally mistaken about what that person is really like. People usually partly conceal themselves by what they say; they lie and deceive. God would not do that, of course. Yet the verbal content of a speech must be distinguished from an actual event of speaking (to which very few people can have direct access); and any act of speaking must be distinguished from the complex, and largely hidden, person who performs that act. So if we are to think of divine speech as disclosing, making present, the actual being of God, there must be some way of ensuring that the encounter is authentic and is understood correctly.

Barth points out that we would need a special sort of insight to understand a revealing speech, and this is where the next element of his account of revelation comes in. The third element proposed by Barth, 'revealedness', is not usually part of the concept of revelation in general at all. A revelation exists, usually in the form of words. Whether anyone understands or notices those words or not, or the extent to which people understand the words, is irrelevant to the occurrence of the revelation. God causes truths to be uttered. But they might not be noticed by more than a few people, and even those people might interpret the truths very differently. So the reception and understanding of revelation is not part of the concept of revelation itself.

God must open the eyes of sinful humans for them to be receptive to the revelatory speech. Barth proposes that it is God in person (as Holy Spirit) who gives us this understanding. The Spirit is the 'Yes to God's Word spoken by God for us . . . also in us' (Barth, 1936, p. 453). This element does not occur in accounts of religious revelations in general, and it points to the distinctively Christian idea that Barth is in fact expounding. When Barth says that God reveals 'Himself', he has in mind the doctrine of the Incarnation, that God's revelation is a person who is identical with God. When Barth says that the reception of revelation in a human

person is a 'self-impartation' of God, he is thinking of the Holy
Spirit as operative within humans to unveil the truth of God to
them. It is the Spirit working within humans who makes God
present and known, and so the act of revelation (the life of Jesus)
only becomes true 'revelation', an unveiling of divine presence,
when God in person makes it happen in the lives of particular men
and women: 'Revelation is a concrete revelation to concrete men'
(Barth, 1936, p. 325).

Thus for Barth, revelation is an event in which God makes
himself present and makes that presence known by acting within
human minds to enable them to recognise that presence. It is not so
much that 'revelation', as a general idea, is the root of the doctrine
of the Trinity. Rather, faith in Christ suggests a very distinctive
idea of what revelation is: God manifesting in Jesus as 'God a
second time in a very different way' (Barth, 1936, p. 316) and being
recognised and acknowledged as God by the illuminating power of
the Spirit, which is not at all under human control.

I think that Barth is importantly right in thinking that the
Christian Trinity could only arise from, and depends upon, revelation and not a general philosophical world view. He is right in saying
that the heart of Christian revelation lies not in a series of propositions but in the living person of Jesus. Christian revelation depends
upon acknowledgement of Jesus as the human embodiment of a
transcendent God, and upon acceptance of the ongoing activity of
the Spirit as the one who makes that embodiment present to and
effective for spiritual liberation in the lives of millions of human
beings. It should never move far beyond that point of origin.

But we should note that on this account the 'seeing' of God
which takes place in the revelatory encounter may, and does,
take many different forms in different people and it is rarely, if
ever, clear and fully adequate. This will inevitably be the case if and

to the extent that 'revealedness' is included in the concept of revelation itself. For what people think is revealed to them will often differ substantially both from the original 'revelation' and from what others think is revealed to them personally. To that extent, this sort of Christian revelation is ambiguous and almost always capable of further development. It will not be conceptually clear and precise, and it need not be conceptually developed at all. Barth is of course aware of this, since he courageously opposed large numbers of German Christians in his own life. Nevertheless, it is important to bear in mind that claims to have encountered the real and living God, and to have had one's mind illumined by the divine Spirit, carry no guarantee of inerrancy.

CHAPTER 13

Hegel and Modern Theology

There is a certain irony in the fact that, though Barth constantly decries the influence of philosophers on faith, the terms in which Barth spells out his 'event' view of revelation are strangely reminiscent of Hegel, the author of one of the most ambitious philosophical world views there has ever been.

When we read that 'God the revealer is identical with His act in revelation and also identical with its effect' (Barth, 1936, p. 296), it sounds as if God speaks primarily to himself and that when God speaks to us, only God, existing in us, understands what he says. Humans become the vehicles of an internal divine soliloquy whereby God expresses himself fully (in human form) and understands himself truly, by interpreting that self-expression correctly from within human minds. Humanity (true humanity, in Jesus) becomes the means of God expressing and knowing himself fully. That is an almost exact statement of Hegel's thesis that Absolute Spirit (*Geist*) expresses and objectifies itself in human history and comes to realise and know itself fully through incorporating that historically achieved knowledge into the eternal divine being.

Such an interpretation, made explicit, would no doubt horrify Barth, as it makes humanity necessary to God's self-manifestation and self-knowledge. Yet Barth does hold that the Son is eternally decreed to become incarnate, and to include humanity in God. So even though this eternal decree is, Barth says, freely made, it does seem to make humanity in some sense necessary to what God essentially is.

My point is not that it is a terrible thing to be Hegelian but that perhaps a specific philosophical system is more important to Barth's theology than he acknowledged. I would want to distinguish God more clearly from His act of revelation, which takes place in the created world and so cannot be part of the divine essence. And I also wish to distinguish more clearly the revelatory act (the life of Jesus) from its reception by humans and distinguish that reception, or its many diverse human receptions, from the self-understanding of God or from the self-understanding of the Spirit as it responds to God from within human lives.

If you do that, however, you begin to move away from an essentially Trinitarian interpretation of revelation. For revelation is not part of the divine essence, and therefore it may be a symbol or a manifestation rather than a disclosure of the divine essence – as Barth says, even in the Incarnation revelation occurs 'in the form of something He Himself [God] is not' (Barth, 1936, p. 316). It is hard to see how this is compatible with saying that in Jesus God reveals 'Himself' as God truly is. And the way in which revelation is received, interpreted, and understood may be a purely human matter and not one which involves God in any substantial way.

I am not denying that Jesus is in some sense identical with God or that the Spirit does inspire and enable human apprehensions of God. But these beliefs depend upon a specifically incarnational understanding of God and not on a concept of revelation as such. As far as revelation itself is concerned, there is no need for God to be Trinitarian for an event of encounter with a personal god to occur. Martin Buber makes such I–Thou encounters central to his clearly non-Trinitarian view of God.

It may also seem that an account of revelation as an event of encounter with the very being of God, enabled by the Holy Spirit, is unduly subjective – another accusation that would appal Barth! The problem is that any claim to have encountered the essential being of God, who is on all sides admitted to be ultimately hidden and incomprehensible, seems almost absurdly arrogant. And such a claim is not helped by the mere assertion that it is God who ensures this encounter, because of course it is only one's own opinion that God does so – an opinion that would immediately be countered by Muslims, Mormons, Jews, and many others! Similarly, any claim that the Holy Spirit has succeeded in authentically delivering such an encounter runs into the difficulty that many different Christians assert so many conflicting deliverances that it is hard to say why one should believe one of them in preference to the others, simply on the grounds of the claims themselves.

The upshot is that, while Trinitarian belief is founded upon the revelation of God in the face of Jesus Christ, this cannot license claims that such revelation discloses the essential nature of God as it is in eternity and as it is unchangeably bound to be throughout all times and places. It cannot justify a belief that this tradition alone identifies God truly and adequately. There is a claim that Jesus really does reveal God's nature and purpose for humanity and that the Spirit can help us – though probably only partially and tentatively – discern what this is (to interpret Jesus adequately). And there is a claim that this revelation of God to us (to us, so puny, ignorant, and peripheral even within our own universe!) is finally definitive of ultimate reality, throughout every possible universe or even apart from our existence or the existence of any created universe. The first claim is part of Christian faith, and our acceptance of the revelation of God in Jesus may be said to justify it. The second claim is one that this revelation cannot support – and that it may be unwise to make.

CHAPTER 14

The Immanent Trinity

Barth would claim to derive the doctrine of the Trinity from Scripture, but he admits that nowhere does Scripture say anything like this. In the Old Testament, usually God refuses to reveal himself ('No one shall see me and live', Exodus, 33, 20). God reveals statutes and ordinances, but not Godself. In the New Testament of course Christians see Jesus as a manifestation of God in human form. But can it be credibly said that Jesus reveals everything about the nature of God? If so, why have there been so many arguments about it ever since? If we see Jesus, we see the Father, according to John's Gospel (John 14, 9). But no one thinks, I hope, that the creator of worlds looks like a young Jewish male. The word 'see' does imply that we meet the Creator in some form if we truly encounter Jesus. There is a sort of 'event of encounter' view at work here, and it is by the aid of the Spirit that we see Jesus as the human form of God. But it is important to say that we do not see God in Jesus clearly and in a form that could never be surpassed – there have been too many interpretations of Jesus as sexist and nationalistic, or as stern and judgmental, or as passive and ascetic, for that to be plausible. Jesus may embody God as fully as any human person could; but we, as individual human beings, do not always see that, for even the Spirit does not work in any of us in such a way that it renders us sinless and perfectly wise.

Barth acknowledges this. He says repeatedly that in speaking of the Trinity 'we do not know what we are saying' (Barth, 1936, p. 441). So perhaps he would not castigate me too much for saying that he sometimes says things that might be better left unsaid. What I have in mind specifically here is his insistence that the divine persons exist 'antecedently' in themselves, in the way in which they appear to us in revelation. For example, in revelation history the Father loves the Son and the Son obediently loves the Father in return, and the Spirit is the form in and through which Father and Son are inwardly united. So, Barth says, this must be true of God in eternity: 'In eternity He is the Father of the Son' (Barth, 1936, p. 394). The Father loves the Son and the Son loves the Father in eternity.

The problem for Barth is that he has already said that there is only one conscious Subject in God, even though it manifests in three forms. It is, I have already argued, possible to say that God loves the divine self in that God both wills and loves (contemplates and appreciates) the Good which is part of the divine being. But God does not love the Good in the same way, or with the same sort of love, as God loves one who is truly other than the divine, or as God even loves other persons who have fallen away from God and frustrated the divine purposes for the world. Divine self-love should not be thought of as egoistic, but it is certainly not centred on a genuine 'other' who may fail to return love and who may stand in need of compassionate help.

The incarnate Son, in his truly human nature, prays to and obeys the will of the one he calls Father. The incarnate Son has a separate centre of consciousness and will, unique in being united to the divine consciousness both fully and from the first moment of his existence. The eternal and pre-incarnate Son, however (the eternal Word), cannot be a separate centre of consciousness, since Barth denies a multi-consciousness account of God. It follows that the relationship of Father and Son in eternity cannot be the same as the relationship of Father and incarnate Son. In fact, as I have suggested, the eternal Word of God is more like a thought or self-expression of God than like another person who can love and be loved. The Father may love (admire, contemplate) his Word (thought, self-expression). But words do not love the one who speaks them.

The problem is compounded when Barth writes that 'God is the one God in three-fold repetition' (Barth, 1936, p. 350). Whereas Jurgen Moltmann thinks that each divine person is a different kind of thing from the others, Barth says that each divine person (or mode of being) 'repeats' the others, which must mean that each is exactly the same in quality as the others. Barth confirms this when he says that the persons differ *only* in that 'They stand in dissimilar relations of origin' (Barth, 1936, p. 363). The Father is unoriginated, the Son has his origin in the Father, and the Spirit has his origin in Father and Son together (Barth accepts the 'filioque' clause of the creeds).

If three persons differ only in how they originated, in what sense could love exist between them? They would each be loving someone exactly like themselves. 'The triunity does not mean that three parts of God operate alongside one another in three different functions' (Barth, 1936, p. 394). So they have nothing to learn from or give to one another. Self-love becomes indistinguishable from love of another, since the 'other' is just oneself repeated. Yet Barth says that Father, Son, and Spirit do have different functions in history. Only the Son suffers and dies. Only the Spirit resides within human persons. Only the Father sends and commands. Barth cannot consistently say both that the divine persons exist in eternity just as they do in history; that they perform different and non-interchangeable functions in revelation history; and that the divine persons are repetitions of one another, alike in all things except for their manner of origin. This is an inconsistent triad of propositions.

There is an unresolved tension in Barth's writings on the Trinity between a truly one-consciousness view and a three-consciousness account, for which real relationship between different subjects seems to be implied. Like many three-consciousness accounts, the Holy Spirit becomes a sort of test case. Is the Spirit a distinct subject of consciousness and will or not? For Moltmann, it clearly is, and Moltmann protests that Barth's account fails to affirm this. Barth holds that Father and Son are persons between whom mutual love exists. That is at least a bipersonal view. But what of the Spirit? The Spirit, writes Barth, is 'the fellowship, the act of communion, of Father and Son' (Barth, 1936, p. 469). An 'act of communion' or 'fellowship' is not a subject of consciousness. There could be a person who unites two other persons, but why should that be necessary? The act of uniting itself is an impersonal event, something done by a person, or perhaps by two persons. Why does there need to be a distinct act of uniting two forms of the divine being? Barth says that 'the fellowship between Father and Son' is 'the essence of the Spirit' and that it is a 'prototype of the fellowship' between God and human beings (Barth, 1936, p. 482).

It makes sense to say that fellowship (union) between God and humans could only be accomplished by God and that God might work in a special way, immanently within human lives, to establish and sustain such fellowship. However, it does not obviously make sense to say that there is a fellowship between two persons within God which needs to be effected by a third person within God. Nor does there seem to be any reason that there should be a prototype of divine-human union within the being of God. For within God there is no real 'other' to be united and no need of any power greater than one's own to effect the union.

All these problems arise from trying to assert that the immanent, eternal Trinity must be identical with, or a sort of internal model of, the economic, revealed Trinity. That, however, almost forces one to adopt a three-consciousness – or, I have suggested, in Barth a bipersonal plus a third impersonal element – account of the Trinity. If we are to speak of God as one personal subject in three modes of being or manifestation, there is no reason to suppose that these modes, which truly exist as God relates to humanity, exist in just the same way in God *in se*. In fact, as I have argued and as Orthodox theologians often said but rarely pressed to its logical conclusion, there is good reason to suppose that the God of a hundred billion galaxies will be far beyond human imagining. Maybe, just as we should stop thinking that Jesus will literally rule the earth one day and that all other religious beliefs will collapse except the Christian, so we should stop thinking that Father, Son, and Holy Spirit is the one finally true identifying name of God for every inhabited planet in every galaxy and universe (as John Zizioulas, for example, has asserted).

We can affirm that Jesus truly reveals God as unlimited, unitive wisdom and love. Jesus is the embodiment of divine love on this planet and the one who suffers and dies as a man that we might be united to (made one with) God. We can affirm that we and all creatures can be united to God by the power of that divine love, a power which is known to us as the Spirit of Christ. And we can affirm that God is the personal creator of the universe, who wills that the universe will find its true fulfilment in union with the divine. Thus we might say that there is indeed a cosmic Trinity and that it has disclosed itself to us in ways suited to our under-standing – as Father, Son, and Spirit. Whatever we discover, and whatever hitherto unimagined worlds we may confront in future, this can remain an unchanging ground of Christian faith. But it does not entitle us to say that the way in which God truly appears to us is the way in which God must appear to all possible beings or the way in which God is in the divine being itself, apart from any creation.

CHAPTER 15

The Identity of the Immanent and the Economic Trinity

One main reason many theologians have been persuaded that God must be as God appears to humans is to be found in Karl Rahner's *The Trinity*, first published in 1967, which contains the 'Rule' that 'The "economic" Trinity is the "immanent" Trinity and the "immanent" Trinity is the "economic" Trinity' (Rahner, 1979, p. 22). As Rahner goes on to expound it, this rule means that there is one God in three forms of subsistence (very much as in Barth), both in relation to creation and considered in itself alone. It is in that sense that the Trinity is the same both in itself and in relation to creation. This leaves other senses in which the economic and immanent Trinities are different. For instance, the Trinity without creation would obviously have no relations to non-divine entities. It would not enter into created reality, redeem others or sacrifice itself, or include created beings within its own nature. It would presumably not suffer or take risks or exhibit compassion, and it would not unite itself to human nature as it is thought to have done in Jesus. In all these ways the immanent Trinity would not be identical in its acts or in its forms of subsistence with the economic Trinity.

Why, then, does Rahner insist on identity in this case? It seems to be because he thinks that if there were no such identity, 'That which God is for us would tell us absolutely nothing about that which he is in himself' (Rahner, 1979, p. 30). The way God appears to us in Jesus would tell us nothing about what God really is. This, however, seems a huge overstatement. As far as we can tell, God could very well tell us much about the divine being without actually appearing to us at all. For instance, God could reveal in words that God is the creator of everything but Godself. That would tell us something very important about God, but sets of words are not at all identical with the being of God.

In fact, Rahner is working with a special sense of divine revelation, very like that of Barth, as divine 'self-communication'. God communicates not a message or even a likeness (say, a human image of the divine) but the 'self', the very being, of God, and this self is received by God as Spirit in the being of those who receive the revelation. God's self may thus be communicated by God and received in creatures; but even if there are no creatures, if God exists without creation, Rahner holds that God still communicates the divine self. That self is given, 'received', and loved by God. So God 'mediates himself to himself' (Rahner, 1979, p. 102).

It is the notion of God mediating himself to himself that is fatally obscure. Persons can reveal themselves in their actions, which can show what kind of persons they are and what their purposes may be. It makes good sense to say that Jesus, by his actions, his teachings, and his sacrificial death, can be correctly taken to reveal the nature of God as self-sacrificial love. In his resurrection, Jesus can show the purpose of God to transfigure human beings and unite them to the divine life. The human nature of Jesus, for orthodox Christians, is united to the eternal Word, which is indeed glorious and unlimited in goodness. So we can speak of Jesus as God's self-communication in that he makes God present in the human world and is the vehicle of God's action in that world. This, we might say, is an appropriate form of subsistence of the divine self, as God enters into relationship with a created world.

But this is different from the picture presented by Rahner: the immanent Trinity of God possessing the divine reality; uttering or expressing it so that it exists alongside the primal source as the same divine reality, but in a freely given and generated form; and the same divine reality as appropriated, known, and loved as actually present in and loved within some form of consciousness. There are not, Rahner says, three consciousnesses or spiritual centres of activity (Rahner, 1979, p. 106). 'There exists in God only *one* power, *one* will, only one self-presence, a unique activity, a unique beatitude, and so forth' (Rahner, 1979, p. 75). But this oneness is not a 'lifeless self-identity without mediation'; it is being which objectifies itself and knows and loves itself in that objectification, and so has a threefold manner of subsistence.

There is, however, little reason to think that this Being has to objectify itself in order to know itself and has, in addition, to objectify itself a second time in order to love itself. The idea of a self-communication of being within the Trinity has little to recommend it. It is a sort of unnecessary inner duplicate of the self-communication of God to other beings via the economic Trinity. The Being may well express itself in finite form in order to be known by finite persons and may act within the inner lives of created persons in order to unite them to the divine. But there is no reason for such expression and action within the life of God in itself. In other words, the attempt to identify the economic with the immanent Trinity through the idea of self-communication, or a mediation of the divine being to itself, is not convincing.

CHAPTER 16

Hegel Again

As with Barth, it is instructive to compare Rahner's view with Hegel's picture of 'being-in-itself', which comes to knowledge of itself by objectifying itself as 'being-for-itself' and then unites this objectified being to its primal origin, thus fulfilling in time its eternally complete being as 'being-in-and-for-itself'. Hegel took the doctrine of a threefold God and transmuted it into a grand picture of the whole of reality as the story of Absolute Spirit progressively coming to know and love itself in and through the history of the world. Rahner seems to be taking the Hegelian world picture and compressing it back into its Biblical origins as the story of one man who uniquely expresses being-itself, and one Church which uniquely appropriates and mediates the divine love as seen in Jesus.

The picture is not, in Rahner, compressed in such a way that the rest, the non-Christian part, of humanity is excluded from 'the self-communication of God to man' which 'must present itself to man as a self-communication of absolute truth and absolute love' (Rahner, 1979, p. 93). One might say that, for Hegel, the whole history of humanity expresses the Absolute. For Rahner, history is largely the story of human failures and aberrations. God must appear in history as a self-sacrificial redeemer, as one preserved by grace from moral evil, as in one sense truly human and yet as uniquely exceptional, as one fully united to God by a unique act of divine power. For Hegel, at least on some interpretations of his difficult writings, each individual person is a moment in the self-expression of the Absolute. For Rahner, individual persons are free and responsible, and are invited to share in eternal life without losing their separate identity. They must freely accept the divine love they are offered, and so there must be a community, founded on God's self-revelation in Jesus, which mediates that offer to people in many different places and at many times. Absolute truth and love may be definitively revealed through one community (or set of communities), but the revelation is precisely that such truth and love are universal. The Church shows that universal love is the deepest character of reality, and precisely by showing that, it shows that such love is not confined to the Church – or, we may add, even to one species or one planet in the cosmos. Thus Rahner's picture of divine revelation in Christ is not an exclusive one only for the few who are privileged to receive it. It is a universal Gospel of salvation, though it is mediated by one specific historical person and the community founded in his name.

For Hegel, self-objectification and self-reconciliation are necessary because being-in-itself is abstract and without knowledge or feeling. The world is necessary for it to become what it is; the world is an essential part of its being. And the world has to be integrated into absolute being in order for being to achieve the realisation of its potentialities. The divine has to express itself and fulfil its inner potentialities in the world in order to be what it truly is.

That, however, has not been generally thought to be true of the Christian God, who is not abstract but fully real in itself, not needing the world in order to be fulfilled (though it may be that God 'needs' a created world in order to express the divine nature as specifically agapic love). It is when created persons are brought to be that a good other than God might be realised in the world by divine action, perhaps uniting finite and divine in a creative union of wills. And finite persons could be brought into this union by the action of God working within them to shape them progressively towards their own unique forms of the ideal.

This is the work of the economic Trinity. Jesus does express the being of God in time, and the Church does mediate the action of the Spirit that unites humans to the divine. But these are essentially temporal and relational properties, and they cannot simply be carried over into eternity, into the life of a God who is beyond the time of this cosmos. What God is in time, God truly is. What God is beyond time, we can only speculate. Despite what Rahner says, they cannot be the same thing.

Rahner's account of the Trinity is illuminating with respect to God's being and action in relation to creation (the economic Trinity), but when he comes to speak of the immanent Trinity, he relapses into a speculative sort of Hegelian metaphysics. Rahner writes, 'An authentic metaphysics of the spirit tells us that there are two (and only two!) basic activities of the spirit: knowledge and love' (Rahner, 1979, p. 116). Consequently, he writes about 'The intra-Trinitarian processions, of which there necessarily can only be two' (Rahner, 1979, p. 93). I do not think this claim can be justified. There are many ways of speculating about the nature of Spirit, and which one is authentic cannot be decided in any neutral way. You could think about Spirit, as I have, as knowing, willing, and loving, for example – three basic activities. There are no doubt many other basic activities that one might add too, such as imagination, or wisdom, or beatitude. There is no a priori way of deciding how many 'processions' there may be in a divine being.

This is where one needs to say that it is Christian revelation that generates a threefold description of God, and exactly what constitutes the 'three' will depend upon how that revelation is understood. Rahner seems confident that it is natural to see Christ as expressing divine knowledge or truth and the Spirit as expressing divine love. But in the Gospels what Jesus expresses above all is God's agapic love. True, Jesus is also described as 'the truth' and as the Word of God, but it is his life which provides the ideal pattern of an *agapic* life. It is the Spirit who is called 'the spirit of truth', who leads into all truth. Love is one of the fruits of the Spirit, but the New Testament speaks more often of the Spirit as advocate, inspirer, and strengthener than as an expression of love. It does not seem right, looking at the Biblical descriptions, to say that the Son expresses divine knowledge and the Spirit expresses divine love. It is almost exactly the other way round. We should perhaps really say that Son and Spirit both express divine wisdom and love, but in different ways – one in a fully inspired man, an ideal pattern of human life in God, and the other as a dynamic process present in many imperfect hearts and minds.

So is God without creation not Trinitarian? That is not what I am saying. I am saying that God is truly known by us in three forms of subsisting or acting. Of God *in se* we can only speculate, and our speculations must always be tentative and based on what we think to be necessary for God to be threefold in relation to created beings. I do think, however, that Rahner is wrong to say that the immanent Trinity must be identical with the economic Trinity. Rahner's model of the existence of self-communication or self-giving within the Trinity can also be misleading. For, despite the fact that he insists on only one will and power in God, the picture of the Father giving himself to the Son, and the Spirit sharing in their love within the Trinity itself, almost inevitably leads to the thought of a divine society of persons, three consciousnesses and wills in God. That view I find too close to tritheism for comfort and too susceptible to a one-sided, almost-masochistic view of love as total self-giving which neglects the important fact that fully realised mutual love is intrinsically and mutually fulfilling.

CHAPTER 17

What Creation Adds to the Trinity

My argument thus far implies that the existence of an economic Trinity, which entails the existence of a created world, adds something to, and actually changes, the being of God. It enables us to see God as contingent and creatively free in actualising ideals of goodness for this cosmos and in bringing into being finite, cooperative creators and contemplators of new values. In this way, this cosmos generates new values of relational creativity which logically could not exist in God alone. The creation of a universe will change God and add something quite new to a postulated immanent Trinity – a God without creation.

This supposal is based on what I take to be the distinctive insight of Christian faith that the union or communion of the created order and the divine is the distinctive purpose and goal of creation. God creates the cosmos and gives it creative autonomy as conscious agents emerge within it, and as such becomes 'Father of the Universe'. God is manifested on the planet earth in the particular form of the fully human person of Jesus, and as such becomes 'Son of the Father'. This is a focal and decisive moment in the process of uniting finite human beings and the divine, a process which is carried through by the Spirit.

Seeing God as Trinity in this way involves belief in, and is in fact a way of formulating, the cosmic goal of union between finite persons and the divine. And it implies a specific view of the personal nature of God. Because of Jesus' peculiarly intimate relationship with the creator, God is known as his 'Father'. God is thus not seen as a remote and rather impersonal reality (a Platonic 'Form of the Good' or even the Thomist 'Pure Form of Subsistent Being'). God is responsive and interactive in a personal way and possesses the divine being in relation to the 'other' of created personhood.

It is in this respect, I think, that 'God is love' as *agape* (1 John 4, 8), that God gives his being to another, and that God receives from that other a creative contribution to his own being. For the Father accepts Jesus' experiences and actions as his own, and so adds a new form of being and new temporal values to the divine mind. Jesus, as a created human person, is other than God; yet that other is one aspect of a manifestation of God, and thus one with God in an intimate relationship of love given and received. That combination of otherness and unity, of relationship and union, is at the heart of the Christian idea of God. Father and Son are one in that they are both manifestations of one and the same divine Mind. They are other in that the human Jesus has a different mind and will from the eternal Word, though he is united synergistically and indissolubly with the Word.

God gives his being as Son by taking form in the world and accepting the suffering (and joy) of Jesus as his own. God gives his being as Father by actualising a relationship of love towards the human mind and the will of the Son. This is a sort of self-giving, since it includes human suffering and death in the divine experience. There is love between Jesus and the Father, though it is a slightly different love in each case. There is suffering and change but no risk in the divine love, and there is no possibility of imperfection in the human love.

Nevertheless, it would not be quite right to speak of love between the Father and the Word in its eternal nature, since they are manifestations of the same reality, and that would be a sort of self-love. Relational love can only exist between the eternal Father and the human Jesus – or, we could say, between the eternal Father and the human aspect of the eternal Word. For two wills and forms of consciousness, each different in kind from the other, are here involved. That relational love cannot be transferred to the eternal aspect of the Word.

What this means is that we should not think of Father and Son apart from creation as exhibiting mutual, relational, self-giving love. Karl Rahner, in a footnote in *The Trinity*, writes: 'Within the Trinity there is no reciprocal "Thou". The Son is the Father's self-utterance which should not in its turn be conceived as "uttering"' (Rahner, 1979, p. 76, note 10). Reciprocal love is possible for God, but it can only be rightly spoken of as existing between God as creator and the finite incarnation of God as redeemer. This form of love can exist in God only when there exists an 'other' who is united to, and in that sense included in, God.

It is the intended destiny of all humans (and in some sense of all creation) to participate in such mutual love. But since other humans are not united indissolubly to God, but are indeed alienated from God by their own actions, God's relational love in their case involves the risk (and the actuality, as it happens) of rejection and refusal. Only through the redemptive action of the Son and the unitive action of the Spirit will estranged humans become, as perfected souls, included in God.

So in God we may say that there are three kinds of love. There is love for the perfection of the divine nature (which is not egoistic, but rather a form of unselfish regard for what is supremely worthwhile). This might be called Platonic love or *philokalia*, love of the good and beautiful. It can reasonably be said to have a threefold form – it involves knowledge, will, and love. But that form is not that of the economic Trinity. There is love for a genuine 'other' which is yet necessarily and indissolubly united to the divine nature, a sort of love that Christians take to exist between God the Father and Jesus and in which we might all hope to participate after death. This is *koinonia*, a fellowship of those whose love is centred on another. And there is love for others who are not united to the divine nature and can turn away from it, though they also can, and God desires that they should, be so united. This is *agape*, the redemptive and self-giving love of God that is manifested supremely in Jesus. It is the characteristic New Testament word for love. All these kinds of love can be given a threefold structure. But it is *agape* and the expression of love in Jesus that is the foundation of the Christian doctrine of the Trinity, and that is the sole and distinctive prerogative of the economic Trinity.

CHAPTER 18

The Epistemic Priority of the Economic Trinity

The Roman Catholic lay theologian Catherine Lacugna stresses the epistemic distinctiveness of the economic Trinity, even though she quotes Rahner's Rule with approval. I think she means that it is not the case that God *in se* is completely unknowable (as in some traditional Orthodox theology) or that God *in se* is simple, changeless, and self-complete (as in some traditional Latin theology), whereas God in relation to us is dynamic, personal, and relational. 'God for us is who God is as God' (Lacugna, 1991, p. 305). God in relation to us is disclosed as personal, free, self-giving, and loving, and that is how God really is. There is nothing more and other than that. In this respect, the immanent Trinity speaks of the same God as the economic Trinity.

She argues, however, that Rahner's Rule is not wholly clear. You could interpret the identity of immanent and economic Trinities as saying that there are no properties that one aspect has that the other lacks. That would be, in effect, to say that there is no distinct immanent Trinity. There is only the economic Trinity, and when we see it we see exactly how God really is. Sometimes Lacugna writes as though this is what she thinks. She denies that 'distinctions in the economy originate in and are grounded in distinctions in God' (Lacugna, 1991, p. 221). That sounds as if there are no hidden distinctions in God which give rise to the divine relations to us. God's relations to us constitute what God is. That sounds like a form of direct (sometimes called naive) realism, which states that what we see is exactly what exists. So there is no such thing as an immanent Trinity in addition to and different in any respect from the economic Trinity.

This view could be pushed even further, and sometimes Lacugna seems to do that. She says, 'God's being-in-relationship-to-us is what God is' (Lacugna, 1991, p. 250). It is not just that God is always like what we see or experience God to be. Rather, there is nothing more to God than what we experience. That would mean that God was always in relation to us. Creation, and even the creation of humans, becomes necessary to God, and God could not exist without being in relation to human creatures. If God relates to us by redeeming us and uniting us to the divine life, and if that, and only that, is what God really is, then God has to be always redeeming and uniting creatures. God would not be God without relation to humans. Lacugna sometimes writes as though this is what she intends, but I do not think it really represents her position.

A more subtle position is that we should not deny that God may be more and other than we know, but we are unable to say anything about that – a form of ontological agnosticism. So Lacugna writes, 'There is literally no basis for the claim that God would be one way or another apart from creation, since we are unable to prescind from the fact of creation and our place in it to attach any meaning to the assertion' (Lacugna, 1991, p. 176, footnote 93). Mystery remains important to God, but we can say nothing about it. This view, however, seems to conflict with her denial that God *in se* is unknowable, so it too probably does not represent her final view.

When she speaks about the ontology of personal being, she proceeds more boldly, writing of 'God who is alive from all eternity as a dynamic interchange of persons united in love' (Lacugna, 1991, p. 354). There is a being of God apart from our experience of it.

We can only speak of that being in terms derived from our experience. But that enables us to say that God is essentially a three-consciousness communion of persons. God could perhaps exist without creation, and certainly without us, but God would still be essentially threefold – Father, Son, and Spirit – and would still be personal, free, and loving.

This is, I think, more like what Lacugna wants. Discussing the writings of Schoonenberg and Congar, she accepts that there must be some lack of exact ontological identity (Lacugna, 1991, p. 219) between a God without creation and God in relation to creation. God cannot redeem if there are no fallen creatures to redeem. God cannot unite if there are no creatures separated from God. God cannot become incarnate if there is no world to become incarnate in. So can it be true (as she says) that there is no 'ontological distinction' between God *in se* and God in relation?

God must be doing different things if there is a world of distinct and fallen creatures than God would be doing if there were no such world. Of course you can say that God always has the *capacity* to love and redeem, and in that sense would be the same God. In that sense Rahner's Rule is trivially true. The question is whether God-with-creation and God-without-creation exhibit different properties and whether these properties are different in kind.

Though she may interpret it in rather different ways at different times, Lacugna wants to say that the being of God is essentially relational. She says that 'An isolated person is a contradiction in terms' (Lacugna, 1991, p. 288). This can hardly be said to be a Biblically revealed doctrine. It is not, in fact, a contradiction in terms, though an isolated human person can be a rather sad thing – except, ironically, in the case of a hermit or religious recluse. And in the unique case of God, the one and only creator of everything other than itself, isolation might be bliss, since God would presumably enjoy unlimited bliss in the contemplation of infinite perfection (and that would not be selfish, since there are no other realities in existence). What would be wrong with that, or what would be ontologically impossible about that?

One might say that all being depends for its existence on a personal (conscious, knowing, willing) reality. That is just normal theism. What Lacugna does not like about this is that persons, she thinks, have been construed traditionally as 'centres of consciousness', which she interprets as self-contained substances. The paradigm she rejects is Aristotle's God as 'self-thinking thought (*Noesis Noeseos*)', complete in itself and unrelated to anything else. In contrast, persons, she claims, are 'toward-another', self-diffusing, ecstatic, free, and loving.

It is true that Aristotle's God is not a person. It is a self-existent, self-complete, impersonal substance, though it has personal properties of knowledge and consciousness. It does seem that the Christian God is more personal than this. In Christ God is revealed as self-giving and loving, as concerned with creation. So it is from the economy (from revelation) that Christians come to see God as self-giving and loving, as centred on others. If human persons are to imitate God, this will make a difference. Humans will not try to be like Aristotle's God – indifferent, self-satisfied, and self-sufficient. They will try to be like Jesus' God – compassionate, self-giving, and centred on others.

It is logically invalid to argue, however, as Lacugna does, that '"God's To-Be" is "To-Be-in-Relationship", and God's being-in-relationship-to-us *is* what God is' (Lacugna, 1991, p. 250). It seems wrong, even rather ontologically arrogant, to say that God essentially is 'Being related to us'. Surely God is much more than that and need not even have been that (we might not have existed). God could have existed even if there never were any human beings.

However, it might be possible to hold that God, if and insofar as God is truly love, must be related to some form of other being. If so, God necessarily creates something other to which to be related. If what Lacugna says at this point is correct, then God cannot, logically cannot, exist alone. That is an interesting possibility, though most Christian theologians have not accepted it. I admit that I am half inclined to accept it, though I draw back at the thought of presuming to know what is necessary for God to be God.

Christian theologians have usually accepted, however, that God the Father necessarily generates the Son and the Spirit, and this seems to be a view that Lacugna accepts. It would explain the need for a Trinity or at least for some sort of 'relation to another' within God. But it would also undermine Lacugna's claim that all we know of God is what God is in relation to a world of genuinely other, created persons (the economic Trinity). It looks as if, as with Barth and Rahner, some sort of diversity and personal relationship is being posited within the immanent being of God. And this threatens any claim that there is only one centre of consciousness and will in God, or that we only know God in relation to creatures, or that we cannot speak of God's immanent being at all.

The most difficult problem for Lacugna is that she wants to disallow speculative philosophical moves when defining the divine nature, in favour of revelations of divine love in Jesus and the Spirit. Yet the postulate that personhood is ontologically primary and essentially relational is precisely a speculative philosophical move. You cannot get that from revelations that God in relation to us is loving. You need to add an argument that how God is revealed to us is how God essentially and necessarily is. While someone may feel this is fitting, it is by no means obvious and can hardly be said to be revealed. All you can get is that this is authentically how God relates to us. What God may be out of such relation is hard to say.

As a matter of fact, the presumption is that God would be different if only by lacking all those specific relationships.

Lacugna moves from a conception of a personal, free, self-giving, and loving God to the conception of God as an internally diverse relation of persons only by adopting the 'Cappadocian' theory that 'God exists as diverse persons united in a communion of freedom, love and knowledge' (Lacugna, 1991, p. 243). God the Father does essentially generate an 'other' (or two others) to whom to give himself and thus exists essentially 'only in persons who are toward one another' (Lacugna, 1991, p. 193). This is held to follow simply from acceptance of the three-fold form of God in Christian revelation. 'On the basis of the Economy, God is understood to be personal and self-giving and to exist as the mystery of persons in communion' (Lacugna, 1991, p. 334).

The difficulty is that the 'others' that God generates within the divine being are not genuine others. They are not creatures, but parts of God. They do not need to be redeemed and united to God, as they are already and necessarily one with God. You can ask, of the Incarnation, 'Did God have to become incarnate?' and 'Did God have to redeem humans in just this way?' If God did not even have to create humans in the first place, the answer must be no. All you can get from revelation is that God chose to become incarnate and to unite humans to God by the power of the Spirit. God might, for all we know, have chosen to create other beings, or to have redeemed humans by other means. So although we might justifiably believe that God really did create and redeem humanity, we cannot say that God had to do this, that God could not have done otherwise. Thus we cannot argue from what God has in fact done to what God necessarily had to do.

This thought is strengthened by a realisation that becoming human and inspiring humans, if humans are contingent creations, cannot be necessary to God. So it is extremely unlikely that terms such as 'Father' and 'Son', which are applicable only to sexually reproducing animals, or terms such as 'Breath (Spirit)', which is applicable only to breathing animals, would apply to God *in se*. God might indeed be threefold in some essential way, but why should that threefoldness be anything like the specific way in which God relates to human beings?

Lacugna is, in my view, on much firmer ground when she argues that divine threefoldness is a characteristic of the economy of salvation and that this is the only access we have to the Trinitarian being of God. When she goes on to argue that 'personhood is constitutive of being' and that God exists eternally as a communion of just three persons, she seems to be letting independent speculations take over from anything that follows from Christian belief in participation in the life of God through Jesus in the power of the Spirit.

Her statement 'There is only the *oikonomia* that is the concrete realisation of the mystery of *theologia* in time' (Lacugna, 1991, p. 223) is what her rich and complex argument makes plausible. Our only access to God as Trinity, and our only reason for speaking of God in the specific threefold conceptuality of Father, Son, and Spirit, is experience of Jesus and the Spirit as modalities of the divine. We cannot say that this is the only way in which God is, but we can say that it is how God truly is for us. The being of God in itself, apart from revelation, is a veiled mystery. The Orthodox fathers tend to speak of the *ousia* of God as so totally ineffable that we cannot truly say even that it is good or that it exists. At the same time, they seem sure that God is essentially Trinitarian, which seems to make God known in some way. I think it is more consistent to say that, though we cannot comprehend the divine essence, we are entitled to say that God is essentially personal and loving, knowing, and creative, because these are necessary conditions of God's appearing to us as God does. The mystery of the divine being is perfectly manifested in the divine 'energies', God's being in relation to creation. And it is our knowledge of God as revealed in Christ and the Spirit that impels us to choose from among the many possible categorisations of the being of God a threefold description. But that is not a valid argument to the conclusion that God exists only in a communion of three self-giving persons, or that persons in the sense of self-giving relational entities are constitutive of and ontologically prior to substances, whether 'isolated' or not.

We may, instead, speak of an 'immanent Trinity' as the primal source of being, as creatively expressed in the actualisation of supreme value, and as blissful contemplation of that value – the threefold God of *philokalia*, the supreme Good. If God is indeed essentially creative and loving, then God may relate to some creation in threefold form as its primordial source (*aitia*), as constituting specific ideal finite forms of created being in relation to the divine (*logos*), and as the one who unites all finite forms to the divine (*synergeia*). This would be a description of God generated from Christian revelation. It would expand the necessarily anthropomorphic images of the Christian Trinity (Father, Son, and Breath) into a more cosmic framework. And it would honour the mystery of the divine being as the one originative source and ultimate goal which is mediated to creatures through many diverse histories which aim at uniting all finite things to the infinite in a communion of fulfilled love.

CHAPTER 19

The Trinity and Naive Realism

Christians worship God as universe-transcending creator and sustainer, as manifest in human form in Jesus, and as the inner spiritual power that unites our lives to the divine life. In a way, this is not difficult or complicated. There is one God, who is known to followers of Jesus in three different forms, ways of being, or modes of existence.

Complications set in when this basically simple statement is turned into a set of unchangeable, precise, and definitive metaphysical descriptions of God's innermost being. The root problem lies in the desire for a naively realistic idea of God. Naive realism is the philosophical view that things as they appear to us must be things as they really are in themselves. If they were not, the fear is that we would be seeing 'mere appearances', or even illusions, and we would not be in touch with the real God.

Naive realism is just one philosophical view among others, and it is not very widely held among philosophers. There are many reasons for thinking that reality as it is in itself is not just the same as reality as it appears to us, with our specific sensory and cognitive apparatus. To take just two often-used examples, when we see the moon looking as if it is only a few inches across, that is not how it really is. When we see something looking red, we know (if we know anything about physics) that in reality there is just an electromagnetic wave of a specific wavelength which our sense organs and brains cause us to see as red. The redness is not an objective property, which exists even when we are not seeing it. But of course it is not illusory or false either. It is exactly how electromagnetic waves appear, and should appear, to beings such as us. For reasons such as these, many philosophers are what they call 'critical realists'. They think there is an existing objective reality that gives rise to our perceptions, but it does not exist exactly as it appears to us. It appears reliably, it does not mislead us, it appears in ways appropriate to our sensory apparatus, but we should not think that we see it exactly as it is in itself.

There is little reason for anyone to be a naive realist. So there is little reason for Christians to be naive realists. Therefore there is little reason for Christians to say that God must be exactly as God appears to us to be. Christians can be critical realists and say that appearances of the divine in Christ do not mislead us but that they should not be taken to present God just as God really is, independently of our knowledge. Human cognitive faculties and intelligence are probably much too limited for naive realism to be true. This is a general philosophical reason for denying that the economic Trinity, the Trinity as it appears to us, must be identical with the immanent Trinity, the Trinity as it is in itself, apart from our knowledge of it. Such a claim is unnecessary for preserving the claim that we have authentic knowledge of God as God relates to us, and it may well seem to be an unduly arrogant claim about human cognitive abilities.

Christian theologians have, on the whole, been well aware of this and have usually held a fairly strong apophatic position with regard to God. Thomas Aquinas, for example, while holding that some statements about God are true ('God is wise', for example), insists that they are not true in the sense in which we understand them (*Summa Theologiae*, 1a, Question 13, Article 2). Words used of God are analogical. They apply to God in a way that we cannot fully comprehend.

Any such view rules out naive realism about God. A naive realist must hold that God is exactly as we understand God. But anyone who holds a doctrine of analogical language about God must hold that, since we cannot understand God properly, God must be rather different than we, with our weak and imperfect minds, understand God to be. What we understand of God may not be wholly misleading, and it is better to assert that God is wise than to deny it. But if we think we know exactly what divine wisdom is, we are fooling ourselves – and transgressing the boundaries of human knowledge.

It follows that if we call 'Father', that is a true statement. But if we think we understand exactly what it means for God to be Father, we are mistaken, and worse, we are confining God to the limitations of our own minds. 'Father' will be applied analogically – that is, in a way that states a truth that we cannot fully comprehend.

It will also follow that we cannot fully comprehend what it is for God to be 'Son' and 'Spirit'. So if we ask questions about the exact relations of Father, Son, and Spirit in God, we are asking what the relations are between three terms, none of which we can fully comprehend. There is no hope of gaining a precise, adequate, or unchangeable definition of such relations.

That does not mean that enquiry into the nature of God as Trinity is useless, that we must just repeat the words without hoping to know exactly what they mean. It means that we need to be tentative and flexible in our enquiry, sensitive to the changing nuances and connotations of the words we use, and reluctant to insist on one set of terms as the only correct ones, as though we understood their (analogical) sense in one unchangeably definitive way.

It may be true that God really is threefold in being. Yet it will always be true, also, that the way we understand this threefoldness will be less than adequate. That entails that God in the divine nature itself will not be identical with the *way we understand* God, even though the terms we use with regard to God may truly (but in a way we do not fully understand) apply to God. That entails that naive realism about God is false. God is not in the divine being as we understand God to be.

What we should also say, however, is that God is such that God genuinely, truly manifests the divine being to us in threefold form. This is an 'appearance', but not an illusion. There is a significant difference between an appearance and an illusion. An illusion is something that we believe to be something that it is not. If we see a mirage in the desert, we may believe it to be a genuine oasis, located where we see it. If so, it is an illusion. 'The oasis seems to be there', we may say, 'but it is actually somewhere else'. Or perhaps we see a rope and believe it to be a snake. That too is an illusion, a false belief. We think it is one thing, and it is another.

Now think of an electromagnetic wave of a specific frequency, which in itself has no colour. But it appears to us as red. Is this an illusion? I do not think anyone would say that. Being red is how that wavelength appears to us, with the sensory apparatus we have. It is a genuine appearance. It is not that it is actually blue but seems to us to be red. Its being red is just how it should appear to beings such as us. The only illusion would be if we said, 'It really is red, even when no one is looking at it'. Thus naive realism about colours is an illusion, a mistaken belief. But we are under no illusion if we say, 'It appears to me as red'. That is exactly how it should appear.

So, if God appears to us as threefold (because of what we believe about Jesus), that is not an illusion. It is not that God is really twofold or fourfold but seems to us to be threefold. God as God is revealed in Jesus should appear as threefold. It is just that we should not fall into the trap of saying that God would be threefold in exactly the same way even if God had not revealed Godself in Jesus.

God has revealed the divine in Jesus. Given that this is true, God really is threefold. This is how God truly and properly appears to us. All we need to remember is that we cannot conclude from this that God, even apart from such revelation, really is just as God has appeared in Jesus. All we are entitled to say is that God is such that God authentically reveals the divine in Jesus in a threefold way.

CHAPTER 20

The Trinity and the Cosmos

I think the foregoing is what some theologians have in mind when they say that we can only know God through Jesus. For we can only know God as Trinity if we start from revelation in Jesus. It does not follow, however, that we can know nothing at all about God apart from Christian revelation. It does not seem sensible for a Christian to doubt that Abraham and Moses knew much about God without knowing anything about Jesus. Many people think that there are good arguments for the existence of a good creator of the universe without any appeal to revelation at all. If God is revealed in Jesus, then God is revealed as Trinitarian. This does not exclude the possibility that God may be revealed in other ways or that it is reasonable to believe in God without any appeal to revelation.

What a Christian is entitled to say, then, is that God is truly revealed in Jesus as Trinitarian. But we do not fully comprehend exactly what this means. We are certainly not entitled to say that God is exactly as we understand God. We need to be rather less arrogant than that. The upshot is that we should never pretend to speak about the 'inner life', the *ousia*, of God as though we could make clear and correct inferences from Christian revelation to statements about what happens in the life of God apart from that revelation. What we can do is to say, 'If God is revealed as Trinity through Jesus, then God must be such that this is a genuine revelation. It shows what God really is in relation to us and our understanding. But God may be infinitely more than that, and in ways we cannot at all understand'.

Does this mean that God is only Trinity in relation to us – to put it in traditional terms, that the Trinity is only a matter of the divine 'economy' (*economia*)?

I doubt if one should go as far as this – and that, perhaps, is Lacugna's problem of wanting both to say that we only know the economic Trinity and that God must surely exist in some way beyond human knowledge of God. If the revelation of God in Christ is a genuine revelation, then God is truly a transcendent creator who unites finite creatures to the divine being both in one paradigm case (Jesus) and possibly through inner spiritual power in all finite persons.

We can infer some things about the eternal God from what God has contingently done. If God has created a specific universe when God did not have to do so, then it is valid to infer that God is free and immensely powerful and wise. If God has become incarnate in Jesus, then it is valid to infer that created and uncreated being can be united and that God has good purposes for creation that God will realise. But can we infer from the fact that God was incarnate in Jesus and is known in many lives as inspiring Spirit that God is essentially and apart from all creation Father, Son, and Spirit? There is certainly no valid deductive inference from the possibility of divine incarnation in some finite form to the claim that such incarnation has to be a 'son'. There is a valid inference, of course, to the claim that God *could be* incarnate in human form, since actuality entails possibility. But there might be many other forms of incarnation, or there might be forms of divine liberation that do not involve incarnation, or there might be no creation in which God as Spirit could be active.

Some theologians are not happy with this thought. Christoph Schwöbel writes that unless God was exactly as God appears to us to be, 'God's revelation could not disclose the divine being in its immanent Trinitarian constitution' (Schwöbel, 1995, p. 7). And this 'implies that the Scriptural witness . . . is irrelevant for understanding the immanent constitution of the divine being'. Robert Jenson, in the same volume, strongly agrees: 'God's true name actually is "Father, Son and Spirit"' (Jenson, 1995, p. 32). 'The Biblical story about God and us is true of and for God himself' (Jenson, 1995, p. 36). Christians are not free, Jenson says, either to transcend that by some independent metaphysical doctrine about God's simplicity or to change the names of God (for instance, as some Christians do, to 'Creator, Redeemer, and Sanctifier').

This is clearly a deeply felt insistence that in revelation we truly know God as God really is and that God cannot be known in any other way. I suggest that these assertions actually lead to the result opposite to what these writers intend. They intend to produce a theology of humility, for they are humbly accepting divine revelation just as (they think) it has been given and not judging it by some independent rational theory. But what they actually produce is a rather arrogant claim that they alone know what God is really like, and that their interpretation of Scripture is the only correct one. They intend to produce a theology of 'free and universal love' which 'transcends every exclusiveness of a biological or social kind' (Zizioulas, 1985, p. 60). But what they actually produce is a supremely exclusive and alienating claim that no one else can truly know God. As Zizioulas puts it, 'Only in the Church has man the power to express himself as a catholic person' (Zizioulas 1985, p. 58) – and by that he means, of course, a fully human person. So unless you are this sort of Christian, you do not know God and cannot be a person in the divinely intended sense. Ingolf

Dalferth even proposes that Trinitarian theism is 'anti-theistic' (Dalferth, 1995), the implication being that Jews and Muslims do not even worship the same God. Whatever this is, it is neither inclusive nor is it a very clear expression of free and universal love.

God is indeed love, and God calls humans to reflect the universal divine love in their lives. Part of such love is the virtue of listening attentively to others and seeking to learn from their different attitudes and ways of life. That involves not presuming that they are wrong from the start, whereas we are just right. It means thinking that they may have worthwhile things to say, insights that we lack. It means conceding that we are not infallible, even in our interpretations of our own Scriptures. It entails genuine humility, which implies a lack of inflexible certainty that we alone are correct – though we should certainly be faithful to our tradition of belief, even when our understanding of it is likely to be imperfect. And it entails genuine inclusiveness, which implies that there might well be other ways than our own of relating to the love of God.

It is a very arrogant assertion to claim to know the 'immanent constitution of the divine being'. What human being could reasonably make such a claim, especially when we are well aware that there are many different beliefs about the divine nature, even among Christians? What we need to claim, and all we should claim, is that we know truly how God is in relation to us and that our knowledge is not an illusion, though it probably contains inadequate conceptual formulations.

CHAPTER 21

Revelation and the Immanent Trinity

God truly is Father, Son, and Spirit as God truly relates to human beings. But just suppose there are non-human beings in existence, whether angels or alien life forms. Would God truly be to them a male member of the species *homo sapiens*, his male offspring, and a being which often takes the form of a bird? You may rightly say that it would be a travesty to think that any educated Christian thinks that is what the Trinity really is. Yet in Christian art, God is often depicted as a bearded male and the Spirit as a dove. These may be just symbols, though sometimes even theologians seriously argue that God must only be depicted as male (God, others insist, should not be depicted at all!). The real point is that male gender is a characteristic of bisexual mammals, that the idea of being a son would only make sense where the origin of a life was the result of sexual reproduction, and that birds are one sort of biological entity that may be confined to the planet earth. These symbols could only apply where there was bisexual reproduction and winged flight. Of course they make some sort of sense on this planet, even though they still produce the danger of over-literalist thinking about God. But are we to insist that the only acceptable ways of conceiving a God who has created millions of stars and galaxies are ways that make sense on this small planet? If we are asking about the nature of an immanent Trinity, does it make sense to say that the only acceptable representation is limited to the biological forms existing on a small planet on the periphery of a fairly average galaxy?

Attempts to use expressions such as 'Creator, Redeemer, and Sanctifier' for God are attempts to escape the gender and species limitations of our images of the divine, and they could be understood by many different sorts of intelligent beings, who probably have different specific images of the divine as it relates to them. I am not suggesting that we stop speaking of Father, Son, and Spirit. They are indeed the symbols divine revelation has given us. But should we not also widen our vision, to see that God, not only in the divine being itself but in relation to other beings than humans (or even, perhaps, to other very different humans), is much bigger than can be contained in fairly literal interpretations of our localised symbols for the divine?

In this universe, which need not, most theologians think, have been created, in which there are human beings, who also may never have been created, God takes form as the Son of a Father. But that must be a contingent fact, which might never have been true. Perhaps God has created other universes in which there are very different forms of intelligent life which do not have two genders or genetic inheritance. So there would be no fathers or sons. No one in such a universe would even be able to understand what was meant by calling God 'Father' or 'Son'. The conclusion is that these terms for God, while they may be true, are contingently true. Their actual truth is quite compatible with the fact that they might not have been true of God. Therefore they are not necessary or essential characteristics of God. If so, God might not have been Father or Son but would still have been the same God (would have possessed all the characteristics that are essential to being God).

It also follows that in other universes, or in faraway parts of this universe, it may make no sense to speak of God as Father or Son.

But we should not deny that intelligent persons there would be able to know God (that would be both mean and arrogant). It hardly needs saying that the Holy Spirit would not be representable as a bird there.

If we contemplate the icons and visual representations of the Trinity that exist in so many churches and museums, we must be struck with how very anthropomorphic they are. A male, human-like figure sits on a throne; a young man, often on a cross, is beside him; and a dove hovers over them. The human-centredness of all this is often heightened by having the Virgin Mary represented beside them, as Queen of Heaven.

This might have seemed wholly appropriate when the earth was thought to be the centre of creation and when human beings were thought to be the centre of God's concern with the material world. But can this type of representation survive as wholly adequate when we know that our observable universe is perhaps only a small part of the total universe, which is itself possibly only one universe among many?

From the fact that the universe is unimaginably vast we cannot deduce that there are other conscious, intelligent, creative, and morally free agents elsewhere in the universe. But it is a possibility that there are, and if God is really unlimited in power and wisdom, we might hope that there are.

I am inclined to say that the representation of God as a male human is grossly inadequate, if not actually idolatrous. God must be beyond any finite and physical form, even if God should be thought of as having the mental (spiritual) qualities of knowing, willing, and feeling. Insofar as Christ is divine, that must be true of Christ also. Since Jesus Christ is a union of a finite human nature and the divine nature (or, as I have put it, a unity of a human subject with the form of being of God as participative, as willing to take form in the created world), he will, Christians think, continue to have a glorified human form. But that will not be the completeness of his eternal and divine reality. It therefore becomes reasonable to think that the Word of God could also unite many other finite forms to itself. If there are persons on other planets, we might even expect that this would be so. In other words, the cosmic Word, which is presumably unlimited in nature, can have many finite forms, of which Jesus may only be one. How that could be represented visually I do not know, and it might be better not to try to imagine it. But it might be good if the eternal Word could be clearly distinguished from the human form of Jesus, even though the Word is truly expressed in and is 'one with' that human form.

As for the Spirit, it obviously does not exist as a bird of any sort or as a tongue of flame – two New Testament images. It is quite clear that the visual representation is only a symbol of an invisible spiritual reality. So it is with the Father and also with the Son (since we do not know what the human Jesus looked like, and the figure we see in pictures is a completely imaginary portrait). In short, I think visual representations of the Trinity are misleading, and I am sorry (from a theological point of view) that they exist. Perhaps, however, less anthropomorphic symbolism could be used – for, after all, even words are symbolic representations in a way.

The main point is that the Trinity could be known as such in a huge number of diverse planetary systems, and if there are intelligent beings in such systems, I would expect that it would be. It would be fascinating to find out! The discovery of extraterrestrial life would not throw doubt on our conception of a supreme spiritual being of Trinitarian form, though it might help expand our sometimes rather narrow ideas of God. Heaven may be stranger and more populous, with more varieties of finite beings, than we can imagine or represent. I suppose humans will have a little corner of heaven, however, where Jesus will be King of the human sector and Mary could even be crowned as Queen. It is just that her reign, at least, will be rather less extensive than some Christians have supposed, and Jesus will be known as just the human instance of a divine *Logos* which is expressed in myriad names and forms. There is nothing for Christians to fear in this, and much to expand the imagination and awe with which we see the extent and depth of the divine glory.

What this means is that we should be wary of projecting our knowledge of God, truly revealed to us in Christ, onto the being of God-in-itself. We can only say that God is such that it is possible for God to take Trinitarian form in relation to a creation in which human beings can be united to the divine being by God's self-sacrificial identification with estranged humans. We might well want to generalise this to say that it is possible for God to create many sorts of intelligent beings that are nothing like members of the species *homo sapiens* and may unite any such created intelligent beings to the divine in an appropriate and loving way. God will be essentially creative, loving, and, if necessary, redeeming. But how that will happen we have no idea. And in any case we have moved so far away from the Trinity as it has disclosed itself to humans on the planet earth – as loving Father, redeeming Son, and sanctifying Spirit – that the Trinity we are thinking about, the immanent Trinity, is going to be very different from (but of course not incompatible with) the economic Trinity.

As far as we can see, God only takes Trinitarian form as Father, Son, and Spirit in relation to humans on this planet. But God does truly take that form, which is therefore what we might call a 'capacity essential to the divine nature'. The denial of Rahner's Rule throws no doubt at all upon the fact that we can truly know God as Trinity, that we can do so only in the light of Christian revelation, and that there almost certainly are other ways of knowing God, though under rather different descriptions. It remains absolutely true that, in relation to humans, God is not just imagined or seen as, but really is, a personal reality which truly and essentially has three forms of existing.

PART IV

The Social Trinity

CHAPTER 22

Persons and Substances

In much recent theology, the idea of the Trinity which I have defended, the idea of it as consisting of three 'forms of existing' of the one divine Subject, has been opposed by an influential stream of thinking that prefers to think of the Trinity as a society or communion of three individual subjects – more like 'persons' as they are generally understood. I have suggested that traces of this view can be found in the writings of Barth, Rahner, and Lacugna, even when these writers explicitly oppose it. I believe that this 'social Trinity' idea is more misleading than helpful but that in fact when both social and unitive views of the Trinity are qualified to take account of the unique nature of the Trinity, both views tend to converge, like different metaphors trying to grasp the same reality from different angles. There is, though, good reason to mount a resolute defence of monotheism, and therefore in the end to insist upon a unitive view of the Trinity. That is the case I am going to defend.

In this part I shall mainly consider and criticise the views of John Zizioulas, Richard Swinburne, and Jurgen Moltmann, who have defended a social view of the Trinity. Then, in Part V, I shall argue that the social view and the one-consciousness view are both heavily qualified by their modern defenders, who appeal, respectively, to doctrines of *perichoresis* and of the nature of God as love. I shall conclude by offering a positive account of the essentially threefold nature of God, which is built on acceptance that God is a dynamic, creative, and passionate God who generates an emergent cosmos within which creatively free persons are intended to grow into union with the divine nature, a union foreshadowed in Jesus Christ.

The Greek Orthodox Metropolitan Bishop John Zizioulas has introduced into reflection on the Trinity the thought of some early Orthodox theologians who were relatively overlooked in the West. He argues that the Cappadocian fathers of the Greek Orthodox Church brought about a conceptual revolution in human thought about persons when they formulated a new and distinctive view of the Trinity. This view differs from much in the Latin tradition, which has thought of God as one primary substance with three 'persons' constituted by the divine nature. The Cappadocians reversed this way of thinking by making the persons, or *hypostases*, ontologically primary and thinking of the one God as a sort of 'social unity' constituted by its parts' relationships with one another as persons. This is a view which has become popular in much of modern theology, but I think that it promises much more than it can deliver. It does point to crucially important features of Trinitarian belief. But I shall argue that, unless it is modified so much that it becomes virtually indistinguishable from a non-social view, it is also radically misleading. Much, indeed everything, depends on how the term 'person' is to be interpreted.

What the Cappadocians did was to identify the term 'person' with the term *hypostasis*. The latter term had usually been used as equivalent in meaning to *substantia*, 'substance' in Latin. Aristotle, however, distinguished two meanings of substance or *hypostasis* (in *Categories* and *Metaphysics Z*). 'Primary substance' was an individual thing or bearer of properties, that which can endure through changes to its properties. 'Second substance' was, roughly, a kind of stuff or nature, like 'gold' or 'water'. It referred to a general property (a universal) which can be instantiated in many individual cases.

One thing the Cappadocians did was to run these two meanings together, at least in the case of the Trinitarian 'persons'. Such a person, they said, was neither an individual thing which instantiated a common nature nor just a kind of thing, a universal nature, with no particularised existence of its own. It was a particularised existent which uniquely instantiated a nature which defined that particular, and that particular only. Such a 'person' was not one instance among others of a general nature, which other individuals might share. Instead, each person was logically unique, irreplaceable, and unrepeatable.

The Trinity, on this view, is not, as many scholars have interpreted Gregory of Nyssa, three individuals sharing a common divine nature (despite the fact that he did, unfortunately, use the analogy of three men sharing human nature). Rather, in *The Doctrine of the Holy Trinity*, John Zizioulas writes: 'It is impossible . . . to say that in God, as it is the case with human beings, nature precedes the person' (Zizioulas, 1995, p. 48). Humans share in the kind 'human nature', which logically pre-exists the existence of individuals who bear that nature. But there is not a kind 'the Divine nature' which pre-exists the actual existence of the three persons who constitute God (we are thinking of logical, not temporal, pre-existence). The 'one', Zizioulas says, 'does not precede "the many"'. The persons are ontologically primary. Each person has its own non-repeatable nature.

The concept of 'person' that Zizioulas is sketching here is perhaps distinctively Cappadocian. It is, at least at first sight, an attractive idea, since it may seem that to think of human persons as unique, unrepeatable, and irreplaceable is essential to Christianity and is connected with belief in a personal God who creates humans in the divine image. As Zizioulas says, there may be an important anthropological consequence of such a view, because it may mean, as he puts it, that 'the person cannot be sacrificed or subject to any ideal . . . even of the most sacred kind' (Zizioulas, 1995, p. 56).

It may also be important to say that God, the ultimate reality, is not one impersonal substance, perhaps unconsciously emanating the cosmos. The Latin tradition, epitomised by Aquinas, that God is '*suum esse subsistens*', or self-subsistent Being-itself (Aquinas, 1964, question 7, article 1), in effect identifies God with a supreme Form which is existent of itself and not shared by a number of individuals. But is such a thing personal? It certainly does not seem to be 'a person', since a person, according to Boethius, is 'an individual substance of a rational nature', and Aquinas bluntly says that God is not a substance or a member of any wider class of beings ('God does not belong to the genus of substance': Aquinas, 1964, question 3, article 5). God is self-existent Being, 'Pure Act', and not like any individual object.

The Cappadocians, according to Zizioulas, want the ultimate reality to be not such a seemingly impersonal subsistent Form, but a person, or a group of persons. 'Personhood' is an ultimate and prior ontological reality, and the reality of God is made up of three persons – three beings who are fully and properly persons – who necessarily coexist and together constitute God.

Zizioulas himself points out that for Athanasius and his contemporaries '*ousia* and *hypostasis* mean exactly the same thing' (Zizioulas, 1985, p. 87). So for that Patristic tradition to say that the person is a *hypostasis* would not differ from saying that a person is an *ousia* – that is, that a person is a substance. It is not surprising that the Latins would be alarmed at hearing that there are three substances in God, as that sounds just like saying that there are three gods, three subsistent beings who together form a society called 'God'. It is not surprising, though it is sad, that the Latin and

Greek interpretations of the Trinity began to diverge, even though both insisted that God was Trinitarian. In Aquinas, God could be seen as a combination of Aristotle's primary and second substance. For God will be a Form (second substance) which exists of itself alone (primary substance). God does not exist as one individual case of a general genus of 'gods', or as a genus which is distinguished from others by its possession of distinctive properties. Zizioulas sees this as an impersonal substance, for he thinks that 'persons' are essentially related to other persons and so logically cannot exist alone. Yet the idea of God as an individualised existent which is not a member of any pre-existing class is very close to Zizioulas' interpretation of the Cappadocian idea of 'person' as the instantiation of a uniquely instantiated kind. Aquinas explicitly says that God is not a substance, an individual instance of a class of divine beings. This is because God, being identical with existence itself, cannot be a member of any prior genus. So it would not be right to call Aquinas' God an 'impersonal substance' since that God is not a substance at all.

Still, Aquinas' God seems to Zizioulas to be less than personal, for whatever 'existence-itself' is, it does not seem to be a person or a society of persons. 'Person', as an ultimate ontological reality, Zizioulas defines as unique, free, loving, and relational. If there are three persons in God, there are three quite unique centres of free and loving creative activity who can only exist in relation to each other. Speaking of 'substance' can give an impression of a self-contained and isolated entity which perhaps never really interacts with creation but remains always changeless and impassible. Zizioulas thinks that speaking of 'person' makes the point that God is essentially free and loving. If God is essentially love, then love must exist in God, and so there must be persons who fulfil their own beings in loving one another, and that means God must be a society of loving persons.

Maybe the emphasis on the personal nature of God, as a unique, free, and loving being, not an 'impersonal' Form or self-subsistent and self-contained nature, is more adequate to the Christian revelation of the divine nature. But that does not in itself resolve the question of whether you are talking about God as one personal being or about God as a triad of personal beings. That would require a convincing account of why persons cannot exist alone and of why a personal God cannot relate to created persons without being Trinitarian. I do not think this has been or can be done. I do not think, in other words, that a commitment to the ultimate and irreducible ontological personhood of God entails a doctrine of the Trinity. It can be affirmed without any particular reference to persons within God who love each other, and certainly without any commitment to there being exactly three such persons. Thus, I am sceptical about the Cappadocian interpretation of the Trinity, though I understand the Cappadocian desire to stress the ontological primacy of personhood over impersonal substance.

CHAPTER 23

The Idea of a Personal and Free Creation

Some difficult questions unavoidably arise about Zizioulas' concept of both human and divine personhood. One is the sharp contrast made between the concepts of 'substance' and 'nature' on the one hand and 'person' and 'relation' on the other. Zizioulas says that the concept of 'person' is logically prior to the concept of 'substance'. But this seems a very odd contrast to make. If a primary substance is an individual thing of a specific nature, then a person is obviously a substance. Human persons, anyway, are individuals, substances who are conscious, who think abstractly and act freely (or so it seems to them). They are centres of creatively free acts. There is no reason that all substances should be, as Zizioulas describes them, self-contained, isolated, impersonal, and unconscious. In fact, many of them very obviously are not. The individual substances who are human persons are conscious, importantly related to other persons, and dynamic. So it is not true that persons, as such, are to be distinguished from substances. Some substances will be conscious, intelligent, and free (will be persons), and their nature will precisely include being dynamic, changing, creative, temporal, and relational. It is very misleading, then, to suggest that 'persons' are ontologically prior to 'substances'. But it is not at all misleading to hold that conscious, knowing, and willing substances are not reducible to and are ontologically prior to impersonal, unconscious, and inactive substances.

The United Reformed theologian Colin Gunton agrees with Zizioulas that there has been 'a paradigm shift from natures to persons, from substance metaphysics to a metaphysics of relations' (Gunton, 1995, p. 141). He holds that 'the inner relations of God are free and that God is 'a personal *taxis* of dynamic and free relations' (Gunton, 1995, p. 100), not a necessitarian, substantialist, and static being.

The opposition of 'nature' and 'person' is interesting, and it does mark a change in conceptions of God, though not necessarily in an 'immanent three-consciousness' direction. It is true that the traditional concept of the divine nature in Latin Christianity was dependent on the philosophy of Aristotle. Aristotle's God was a perfect self-contemplating, changeless, and non-temporal being. God was not a creator of the universe, and there was no need for it to create anything, since it already contained all possible perfections in itself, in the most real possible form. Aquinas managed to transmute this self-sufficient God into a creator, since, he held, goodness was essentially self-diffusing. But creation still made no difference to God. Creation arose from a superfluity of goodness, and it left that supreme goodness unchanged and unchangeable.

This is what Gunton has in mind when he complains about this concept of God as the concept of a necessary being which could be otherwise in no respect (so, necessitarian), simple, having no internal or external complexity (so, substantialist), and timelessly eternal (so, static). Gunton is correct in suggesting that the God of the Bible does seem to be a dynamic, passionate, responsive being who guides and reacts to the history of human beings. Even more obviously, Jesus is a historical figure in time who relates personally to other people, and the Spirit moves dynamically in human lives to inspire artistic creation, prophecy, and courage in particular and changing ways. If historical revelation is a reliable guide to the divine nature, the divine life does seem to be dynamic, free, and relational. Robert Jenson, Richard Swinburne, and Colin Gunton all criticise the doctrine of divine simplicity and impassibility by stressing that God is a passionate being who enters into time and thus includes time in the divine being. The point is well taken.

However, this is not really a shift from natures to persons and from substances to relations. It is a shift in the understanding of what a nature and substance is. To have a human nature is precisely to be a rational, creative, and morally free person, and human substances are individuals that have capacities and dispositions to relate to other persons. If God is personal, God also may be creative, relational, and free (whether God will be morally free or not is another question). But there is nothing essentially Trinitarian about this insight. It was after all a Jewish scholar, Abraham Heschel, in his book *The Prophets* (Heschel, 1962), who insisted that the Biblical God was a passionate and responsive, not an impassible, unaffected God.

The analysis of 'personhood' is very relevant to forming an understanding of what the Christian God is like. It is, however, a rather idiosyncratic view of intellectual history to think that our modern notion of 'person' derives from some early Cappadocian concept of 'person'. It seems much more likely that it derives from specifically Enlightenment notions of the radical liberty, equality, and fraternity of human persons, which was often seen as a liberation from traditional Christian ideas, which were often used to justify injunctions to obedience and hierarchy. It may be true that the Cappadocians introduced into the philosophical concept of God the idea of persons as unique, free, loving, and essentially related individuals. But such an idea of personhood is quite compatible with a high valuation of obedience to a hierarchical authority. Indeed, love can very easily be thought to enjoin a self-negating deference and submission. I suspect that the Cappadocian notion of human personhood did so — it was, after all, formed in the extremely hierarchical Byzantine Empire and in a strongly hierarchical church.

Nevertheless, if God is seen as a supreme and loving person (or society of persons), this is rather different from seeing God as the pure Form of existence-itself. If, due to the influence of Greek philosophers, Christians had come to think of God as self-contained, isolated, changeless, and impersonal, it may be a salutary change to insist that God is outward-going, desiring to create and relate to others, and dynamically changing in relation to them. If that is what is meant by saying that the concept of person is logically prior to the concept of substance, then, although it is misleadingly framed, the change is a real and important one.

CHAPTER 24

The Logical Uniqueness of Persons

One feature that is said to make persons ontologically distinct from and prior to substances is that persons, including divine persons, are said to be logically unique, irreplaceable, and unrepeatable – properties which are not supposed to be possessed by 'substances', since substances are instances of a general kind. At least in the case of divine persons, Zizioulas claims that there is no general nature of which a person is one instance. This distinction, however, is logically odd, because every substance is logically unique in that a complete description of any substance, including such things as its position in time and space and its location in a particular universe, will be unique. If this is denied, on the ground perhaps that there could be two complete universes containing qualitatively identical substances, then it will be true of persons, also, that there could logically be qualitatively identical persons in every respect in different universes. So there is not a great difference between persons and substances such that substances are instances of general kinds and persons are not. Despite what Aquinas says, even God, who is unique, is unique because he is the only possible instance of the general kind, 'creator of everything other than itself'. So persons are not distinguished from natures and substances by being the only possible cases of the individuals they are.

Of course there is an important difference between personal and non-personal substances. Persons, but not rocks, have an inner life.

Persons act freely and creatively, and they integrate their experiences in a way that has its own feeling-tone and subjective form of apprehension. Persons are agents and subjects of experience, and are creatively autonomous. It is this inner consciousness and creative freedom which gives persons moral and spiritual importance. That is precisely their nature as substances of a particular kind. Even though I have argued that God is not a person, but is suprapersonal, God may well possess a unique inner consciousness (intuitive knowledge of all possible and actual states) and creative freedom (as creator of everything but itself).

We do not have to draw a distinction between substances and relations, or between natures and persons, to make this point. We can simply say that some substances (some individuals) are conscious and free, and some (including God) are the only possible individuals with the nature they have. So far, we do not have a Trinity, but we do have a stress on the non-reducibility and the priority, both ontological and moral, of personal being. And we have a stress on the uniqueness of the inner life, a spiritual life of subjective appreciation and creative freedom which gives persons special value.

But is the Cappadocian notion of a divine person necessary or even relevant to belief in the moral uniqueness of human persons? The reason I say this is that Trinitarian persons seem, on Zizioulas' account, to be quite different from human persons. As he says, 'In human existence nature precedes the person' (Zizioulas, 1995, p. 48). But that is not true of Trinitarian persons. So human and divine persons are different in kind – in fact, each divine person is different in kind from the others (since they are not members of a genus). This actually creates a problem for Zizioulas' account of the Trinity. He holds that, since persons are ontologically prior to natures, the Father as a unique person is the cause of the Trinity.

The Father is the only ungenerated cause of the other two divine persons. But if divine persons are 'unrepeatable', then the Father cannot give his own nature to the Son and to the Spirit, since the Father's nature will be unrepeatable. It cannot then be true that the divine persons are alike, except in their mode of origin (the Father being ungenerated, the Son generated, and the Spirit 'spirated' from the Father through the Son). Yet, as divine, each person must presumably be omniscient and omnipotent. That means that each person must know everything that the other persons know (or they would not know everything) and that no person can do anything that is not agreed by the other persons (for they must be able to prevent anything they disagree with). In what respect, then, are they logically unique? This problem would not exist if there was only one consciousness and will in God, for then there would only be one unique being who was omniscient and omnipotent.

How far, then, can seeing God as personal, as a conscious, intelligent, and active member of what is a necessarily single-member class ('the creator of everything but itself') lead to a doctrine of the Trinity? So far as the uniqueness and unrepeatability of persons is concerned, I do not think that it can. But perhaps the claim that persons are free in a special sense, or are essentially relational, will prove more effective in supporting a Trinitarian description of God.

CHAPTER 25

The Divine Nature and Freedom

The second major characteristic of 'persons' on Zizioulas' account is that persons are distinguished by their possession of 'absolute freedom'. At least in the case of divine persons, he says that they are not even constrained by having a pre-existing nature to which they must conform. Once again he has highlighted something of great importance to human persons: the reality of creative and moral freedom. We may well want to say that a being without such freedom, or at least without the capacity for it, is not a person. But does it make sense to say that such freedom is 'absolute'? Is that even logically possible? He admits that it is not possible for human persons, who have a pre-existing nature which places a logical limit on what they can do. But he thinks it is possible for, and definitive of, divine persons. But can anything – whether God or the Father, 'the cause of all' – exist without some nature which defines what it is? Even to say that something is free is, after all, to define its nature.

The essence or nature of something is Aristotle's formal cause – what it is or what makes a thing what it is and not another thing. It may seem that everything that exists must have a nature, in this sense. It must be what it is, and not another thing. Created beings all have natures, given to them by the Creator. But the Creator too must have a nature, which is precisely that it is the uncreated creator of everything other than itself. If we believe there is a creator, we know at least that much about its nature, even if there are innumerable other things that we do not know about it.

Theologians sometimes resist the idea that the creator has a nature, on the grounds that God is not the instantiation of a class of things, one object among others which share a property – perhaps the property of 'existing'. I will not enter the debate about whether 'existence' is, in strict logic, a property. It is enough to say that there is a difference between a God who is a fiction and a God who is real and has causal properties, such as causing other things to exist. One God does not exist, and the other does. Even if God exists in a different way from any finite thing, it is true to say that God is not a fiction and is the cause of everything other than God. It is not at all odd to say, then, at least in an informal way, that God has the property of existing.

God, the classical tradition says, is absolutely unique, one of a kind, the only possible member of its class, and so in a sense not a member of a class at all. But 'being unique' is a property too. The truth, logically speaking, is that God is a member of a necessarily one-member class, of the set of logical objects of reference which can possess only one member ('creator of everything other than itself' is such a set; 'being the only self-subsistent Being-itself' is another).

So God has a nature. God in fact will belong to many sets, such as 'the one and only supremely valuable being', 'an omniscient being', and 'a supremely powerful being'. We do not have to be able to spell out such descriptions in detail for them to apply correctly to what we refer to as 'God'.

Does the nature of God belong to God necessarily? That is, could God have been different, not supremely powerful or valuable, or not the creator, or not even existent? Opinions are divided about this. But whatever is the case, it seems that God cannot be coherently spoken of as 'choosing' to have the nature God has. In order to choose X, God would already have to exist and be able to choose between alternative possible states. God would have to know what such states were and have the power to select one. There would therefore already be unchosen properties of God – existence, knowledge, and power. God would either have these properties or not. If not, God could not choose these states. If so, then some states of God are necessarily not chosen by God but already exist in God.

Is God constrained or limited by this fact, by the fact that God does not choose at least these basic states of the divine being – existence, power, and knowledge? I do not think it would make sense to say that. There is not something other than God that causes such states to exist. A fundamental definition of God is usually that God is uncaused. If some states of God are uncaused, then they are necessarily unchosen, since choosing is a sort of causation.

Many philosophers think that things other than God are uncaused and uncausable. For instance, necessary truths – such as truths of mathematics or morality, perhaps – exist, whether or not any universe exists. Necessary truths are uncaused, and since in some sense they exist, they must either be actual in themselves or exist in something actual. For theists God is that actual being in which all necessary truths exist. Since these truths are necessary, God must be both actual and necessary, for that in which necessary truths exist and have their being must itself be necessary. Therefore there is an actual being that necessarily exists and knows all necessary truths.

This being is the creator of everything other than itself. Furthermore, creation is causation by knowledge and intention. God must know what God is creating, and intend to create it. If, as most Christian theologians think, the creation of this world is contingent (the world does not have to be the way it is), God must know many alternative possible and contingent states, and select some to make actual. God necessarily has knowledge of all contingent possibilities and the power to actualise at least some of them (we cannot know which or how many). It follows that God necessarily has contingent powers, powers that God could actualise in other ways. For, as I argued in the very first sections of this book, if God knows something contingent, that knowledge is contingent. And if God can create something contingent, then that creating must be contingent.

Anselm and others, following Plato, held that ideas in the mind of God (including knowledge of all contingent possibilities) are more real than the actual objects that instantiate those ideas. That, however, would make actual existence superfluous and make creation pointless. Also, many possibles represent bad or undesirable states of affairs (the existence of unending pain, for instance). There is a reason for avoiding such bad states, and for choosing good states. We may therefore think that God has a reason for selecting and actualising good states and contemplating them for their own sake. Such actualised good states, together with the complete set of possible states, are parts of the content of the divine mind. In this sense, some creation (some actualisation of good possibilities, even if within the being of God) is necessary for God.

We could say that such necessary creation occurs within the being of God and is not the creation of something truly other than God, something with its own sense and knowledge of independent existence. There need be only one mind that actualises and enjoys these objects of knowledge. God, we may say, is the creator and enjoyer of an everlasting and perhaps limitless set of states (perhaps states of the divine being itself) good in themselves. In this sense God is in some sense personal or mind-like, enjoying happiness in the creation and contemplation of a possibly limitless (infinite) set of intrinsic goods.

Some philosophers (notably, Richard Swinburne) think this is enough to call God a person, since it speaks of a subject who knows, wills, and feels. That would, however, be a very thin notion of 'person'. It would not include any notion of moral responsibility (since God could not do evil) or intellectual discovery (since God would already know everything there is to know) or social relationship (since there are no other persons). It would be very unlike human personhood, and this might serve as a warning that such a conception of 'personhood' should not be too closely modelled on things that are distinctively valuable about human persons. I feel more comfortable calling such a God 'personal', meaning that it is correct to speak of God as knowing, feeling, and willing, and these are all terms we ascribe to persons. Yet God lacks many properties of the entities we normally call persons, such as having a body, moral responsibility, growth in wisdom and knowledge, and social relationships. And God possesses properties that human persons cannot possess, such as omniscience, inerrancy, supreme power, supreme value, and self-existence.

Since God is necessary in existence, knowledge, and power, can we say that such a God is absolutely free? We can, on condition that we think that divine freedom is identical with divine necessity. But this is freedom only in the sense that nothing other than God constrains God to do things against God's (necessary) will. But there is a major problem with this view. For whence, then, is evil? God does not choose evil for its own sake. Yet evil must have its origin in God, since God is the cause of everything other than God. Therefore some things originate in God, but not by choice. They presumably arise by necessity, not by free choice.

Just as God does not choose everything about the divine nature and does not choose necessary truths (being necessary, they are unchosen), so, it seems, God does not freely choose all actualised possibilities. God's freedom (God's fully intentional choice of goods) is limited by necessity (that which arises from God unchosen). God chooses to actualise good states, but some possibles may be actualised by necessity. If evil exists, God's freedom cannot be absolute or unlimited, even though it will not be limited by anything other than the necessary divine nature itself.

It will still be true that the divine being itself is not evil, since an evil being is one that freely and intentionally chooses evil. If some evil arises necessarily from a being but is not freely and intentionally chosen, and if in that being itself only supreme values are actualised, then that being is not evil. In God's own nature there is no evil and no disvalue, such as involuntary suffering. If, however, God chooses to create sentient beings, and if suffering comes upon them not by divine choice but by necessity, then God may suffer by experiencing in some fashion the suffering of created beings. God will not intend that suffering but will seek to ameliorate it and annul it by including it within a wider and overwhelming experience of good. Insofar as this is possible, the being of God can be properly termed wholly good, even though that nature may, by some form of necessity, be the source of suffering in created sentient beings, if and when such beings come into existence.

This might sound like an attempted short way of resolving the problem of evil. But it is not that, at least not primarily. It is an acknowledgement that the evident fact of created evil is a very strong argument against the existence of a God who is wholly good and absolutely free. For being absolutely free means being able to choose whatever God wishes, without any limitations whatsoever. Thus it is a recognition of the logical truth that the divine being cannot be absolutely free. Not only is the divine being conditioned by God's own necessary existence, knowledge, power, and goodness, but it is also conditioned by the existence of necessary truths in logic and morality. From this it follows that there are necessities in the being of God which are not matters of divine free choice. It is therefore possible that there may be something necessarily existent in the divine nature that makes the existence of created evil inevitable or at least unpreventable if specific sorts of created sentient beings are to exist.

We do not know this by any sort of direct knowledge of the divine nature, since we have no such knowledge. But if we suppose that God is the creator of all things, that God intends only good things, and that some bad things exist, we are forced to conclude that God creates (is the cause of) bad things, but does not directly intend to do so. In this case, it might be better not to use the word 'create' and to reserve that word for acts of bringing about intentionally. But we could still say that God 'is the one and only source' of all things, that God intends only good things, so God must be the source of some things that God does not intend. Such things are produced by necessity, and not by will and intention. The argument shows, in my view, that the existence of evil is compatible with the existence of a God who is the source of all things, who intends only good things, but who is unable to prevent the existence of those bad things that are connected by necessity with the realisation of the good things that God does intend.

The stock response to this argument is to complain that such a God is not omnipotent. If that means that God cannot negate necessary truths, that is the case. I have argued, however, that even an omnipotent being will be subject to logical limitations which are definitive of the divine nature. All necessary truths are parts of the divine nature. Therefore even an omnipotent being cannot prevent all evil, insofar as that evil is necessarily connected with the creation of some sorts of overwhelmingly great good. It could be the case that God, who is necessarily the ground of all possibilities, good and evil, moves towards the self-unfolding of ideal potentialities inherent in the divine nature through a process which involves the actualisation of some negative as well as positive possibilities, possibilities which are necessarily interconnected in ways we cannot yet see. 'Omnipotence' can still be ascribed to God, but it must be interpreted as the possession of the greatest possible power, given the necessary nature of the divine as the ground of all possibilities.

The conclusion is that freedom, both in God and in creatures, is necessarily conditioned. This is not a bad thing, for it is better to be unable to hate, to sin, to be stupid, and to cease to exist than to be able to do these things. If one was *absolutely* free, one might actually choose to hate or become stupid, because nothing in one's nature would constrain one to will only what is good. I think that would be an imperfection. So if God is perfect, God must be necessary in a number of respects. These may include, as both Leibniz and Hegel held, the inevitable actualisation of possibilities which 'press into existence' because they are the negative correlates of states or processes which are in themselves good. Such a being is not absolutely free.

CHAPTER 26

Freedom in God and in Creatures

The importance of freedom, in the case of human persons, is that they can choose one of a number of possible states (that is free creativity), and they can choose between self-regard and love of the good for its own sake (that is moral freedom). These are great goods, and much better than their opposites – having no choice about what happens next or being unable to avoid choosing evil.

But such freedom is not absolute. Humans have varying degrees and sorts of capacities: some are good at music, some at craft work, and some at gardening. Humans do not choose to have those capacities, though they can choose to improve or neglect them. Also, the states that humans can choose are limited by the knowledge of what is possible for them in their social and historical context. An ancient Egyptian could not choose to write a symphony – it would simply not be a possibility for ancient Egyptians. But that is not a fact that is freely chosen. Creative freedom lies in making the best of our possibilities and capacities – or in failing to do so. In other words, the greatest freedom lies precisely in finding and realising a role that is proper for us, that is built into our natures and situations and that will realise 'what we are meant to do'. We do that creatively, by developing our capacities in original and perhaps, if we are really good, in unique ways. Creative freedom is the ability to develop in original ways the capacities which constitute our nature. Freedom cannot be absolute, because it consists in creatively developing what we by nature are.

Moral freedom, too, is distinctive of human persons. Moral freedom is the ability to choose between self-regard and altruism, or between love of self and love of good. It is not absolute, because there exists an obligation to seek what is good but an inclination to seek what pleases oneself. Obligations and inclinations constrain human actions, and humans are said to be morally free when they decide to follow one constraint rather than the other. Moral choice is between objective existing possibilities. Such choice is free, but it is not arbitrary as 'absolute' choice would be. The choice between good and evil is a choice between morally weighted possibilities. In making it, the human person determines a way of existence, decides for love or against it.

Neither creative nor moral freedom can belong to a divine person in the same way it belongs to human persons. This applies to God, or 'the Father', if he is a person. God can be creative but cannot develop and make the best of what God is; there is no question of God improving the divine talents by resolve, determination, and hard practice. And God does not have moral freedom at all, since God cannot choose evil. God's choices will always be supremely creative and good. There is no possibility that they could be shoddy or evil. There is no possibility either that God could fail to be compassionate or loving. Therefore God is not *absolutely* free. Yet God may be free to choose between many sorts of good. That is real freedom, and is not limited by the presence in God of inclinations which impede the creation of good. In that sense divine freedom is much greater than any human freedom. Yet it is still not absolute. God creatively expresses what God necessarily is; or, to put it in another and perhaps less paradoxical-sounding way, God necessarily expresses the divine power, wisdom, and goodness in many contingent and creatively new ways. God's being is a perfect blend of necessity and creativity.

Zizioulas posits a severe contrast between 'rational or ontological necessity' and 'freedom'. This reflects a similar contrast he draws between 'nature' or 'substance' and 'free person'. Thus he says that 'the authentic person, as an absolute ontological freedom, must be 'uncreated', that is, unbounded by any 'necessity', including its own existence' (Zizioulas, 1985, p. 43). If what I have said is correct, all freedom must be bounded by the necessity of its own existence, as well as by its knowledge and power. So a total contrast between freedom and necessity is a false antithesis.

One could say that God is absolutely free, in that God fully affirms and wills all that God is in the divine being itself. God is not, of course, free to be anything else. But then God does not, and could not, want to be anything else. Human freedom, in contrast, is not absolute, because human wishes are constrained by and often opposed to the instincts of biological nature. But human freedom can become absolute if, after death and by God's grace, such biological nature is left behind and a new form of existence, the resurrection life, comes to be. In it, humans will be able to affirm everything about themselves without reserve. They will not suffer or experience frustration and temptation any longer. And perhaps, Zizioulas suggests, the Church offers a foretaste of this redeemed future.

In this case, the ontological necessity of having a substantial nature need not, and should not, be opposed to being a free person. They are completely compatible. But then the argument that the concept of 'person' is radically different from the concept of 'substance' or 'nature' falls to the ground. A person will simply be a substance of a specific nature. It will no longer make sense to say that 'nature does not determine the person; the person enables the nature to exist' (Zizioulas, 1985, p. 57). The nature will determine the person as free, and the person will instantiate that nature. There will be no need to say, 'God exists on account of a person, the Father, and not on account of a substance' (Zizioulas, 1985, p. 42), as though persons had no nature and were not substantial things. In other words, the 'Cappadocian revolution' is unnecessary. God may have a nature which is both necessary and free – obviously in different respects.

Necessity and freedom are not the same thing. God may be free in willing the existence of a specific good world. But God is not free insofar as God is the source of evil and suffering. That arises necessarily from God but is not of itself positively willed by God. This is a reason for saying that God is not absolutely free – free from any unwilled necessity. Yet creative freedom is an important property of God, and God possesses a greater degree of creative freedom than any other possible being.

There seem, however, to be no Trinitarian implications of this truth. Indeed, the existence of three divine persons in the Trinity seems to render the absolute freedom of any of them impossible. There is a sense in which the Father is not 'absolutely free'. The Father *must* generate the Son and spirate the Spirit. That is part of what it is to be the Father. There is a nature of God – to be three persons – and a distinctive nature of each person. Zizioulas says, 'the cause or *aition* of divine existence is the Father, which means a person, for this would make the Trinity a matter of ontological freedom' (Zizioulas, 1985, p. 51). But why should that be so? If persons are essentially relational, as Zizioulas holds, then they cannot at the same time be free to be isolatedly individual. Conversely, if they are absolutely free, they cannot be necessarily relational.

How can making the Father the cause of divine being entail that the generation of the other persons is 'not necessary but free'? On the Cappadocian view, it is part of the nature of the Father to be a Father – that is, to generate another person. So the Father is not absolutely free. It is therefore not true that it is an essential (or even possible) characteristic of persons, even divine persons, to be absolutely free. There is no virtue in calling the ungenerated cause of all things a 'person', in the hope that it will guarantee the absolute freedom of the creator of all things. It is illogical to say that the creator must be absolutely free when there absolutely *have* to be three, and only three, such persons and there is no choice at all about it. The conclusion is that arguing for the ontological priority of 'persons' in the Trinity does not help make the Trinity a 'matter of ontological freedom', and it is not possible to make the notion of 'absolute freedom' an internal characteristic of God. If there is ontological freedom in God, it must lie in God's choices of what other things or states to create, not in the (necessary) generation of other persons within the divine being. Freedom is good, and God's freedom is great, but a three-consciousness view of God limits rather than extends the divine freedom.

CHAPTER 27

Persons as Necessarily Relational

I have tried to throw doubt on the claim that persons are logically different from substances, as well as on the claim that persons are absolutely free, though I have agreed that persons have unique inner lives and are creatively (and, in the human case, morally) free. But the most important characteristic of persons, for the Cappadocians, is that persons are essentially relational beings: 'the person cannot exist without communion' (Zizioulas, 1985, p. 18). Persons cannot exist as isolated individuals, and so Father, Son, and Spirit, if they are persons, can only exist in the closest relationship to one another – in communion. The divine being 'precludes individualism and separation' (Zizioulas, 1985, p. 49). The three persons are not individual examples of a common kind, each of which could exist apart: 'none of them can be conceived apart from the rest' (Zizioulas, 1985, pp. 48–49). It is not just that they cannot exist apart; they cannot even be conceived to exist apart.

There is, of course, despite what Zizioulas says, a nature they share – 'being indivisibly one of three'. This marks a great *difference*, not a similarity, between Trinitarian and human persons, who can be conceived apart and are individuals. Human individuals live in society, and that is a very important fact about them. But they can live in solitude; they can live in various different groups, and move to new groups if necessary; they are not indivisibly united to a group of other people. But the persons in the Trinity are so united;

they are essentially relational and essentially related to just two other specific persons. There are essentially three and only three persons united in the Trinity, whereas human persons live in many varied networks of social relationship, which can vary markedly over a lifetime.

It is hard to see why it should be part of the definition of a 'person' that a person must be related to other persons. Of course you can simply make that a prescriptive definition: 'That is what I choose to mean by the term person'. But you must have reasons for recommending such a definition.

If you look up the word 'person' in a dictionary, you will find that a primary definition is simply 'a human being'. If you seek to go further than that, you immediately find yourself in the middle of huge arguments about what exactly is distinctive about human beings, as opposed to other animals. Human beings are embodied animals which live in groups, and which are fairly intelligent. They tend to think of themselves as morally free and responsible. They have language and can think in abstract ways, as in pure mathematics or theology. They can be inventive and creative, and in humans, cultural evolution and development complements or even replaces evolution by natural selection.

The boundaries between being a person and not being a person – say, the boundary between a human and a great ape – can be blurred, but there is little doubt that a mature human has very different mental capacities than those of a gorilla. It is not surprising that Aristotle defined a human person as a rational animal, in which definition 'rational' should be taken in a rather broad sense to include practical wisdom, controlled emotion, and the capacity for cultivating moral and intellectual virtues.

There is no doubt that the cultivation of distinctively human capacities requires membership in society. Human persons start from weakness and ignorance. They learn from others to act and think, what to do, and what language to speak; also what things to like and what to dislike. They discover their own natures by interacting with others, competing, sharing experiences, and cooperating. They act and are acted upon. They assume that others have hidden lives which can be shared or not. They live in societies and cannot normally live alone, without help. We all rely on others to some extent, and we all like to think that our contribution is valued, precisely for its uniqueness. It is important to us that someone cares about what we do, values it, does things to please us, and aims at our happiness and well-being. A little reflection will lead us to see that we should also care for others, do things to please them, and in general aim for their happiness. To live a fully human life is to realise our own personal capacities by interaction with other persons.

Does this mean that human persons are 'essentially relational'? It would be a mistake to dissolve persons simply into their relations or to say that persons are 'nothing but' the sum of their social relationships, as Karl Marx once put it. Social relationships are very important to human persons – though there is no reason all persons should be human persons. We could not be fully human persons without relationships to other humans. But in each person there is a core of individuality evidenced by more than just the ways in which they relate to others. Each person has a unique chain of experiences, a unique responsibility for acting, and a continually developing set of feelings and attitudes that may remain unknown even to his or her closest companions.

I could not play the violin part of a Beethoven symphony unless I was related to others who helped me develop my talents, added their parts to the symphony, and shared my musical experiences. But what that symphony means to me and how it is experienced by me remains a privileged secret of my inner life. So we might well say that human persons are relational – they are properly social animals – but they retain an inner core of unique individuality which is more than the relations which have helped make them what they are. They are certainly not just relations.

It is important to being a human person that we should grow and develop, that we should help others grow and develop (in rearing children, for example), and that we should care and be cared for when other people or we are in need or distress. The relationships in which persons are involved are rich and complex, and they require that others are different from us; that we grow or fail to grow; that we choose the good or fail to do so; and that we experience envy, hatred, gratitude, and love at various times and in often-overlapping ways. Persons need each other because they are unable to exercise their capacities alone. They live with one another in perpetually responsive ways, acting and reacting, constantly learning and adjusting, and negotiating ways of life by perpetual compromise and between relationships of dominance and of submission. Social relationships are varied, diverse, complex, and constantly fluctuating.

Human persons, in a reasonably full sense, are, as Zizioulas says, 'inconceivable without others'. But these sorts of relationships with others are relationships between morally ambiguous, creative and destructive, developing or decaying, dominant or submissive rational animals. Sartre knew that we cannot live without social relationships, and yet he said, 'Hell is other people'. If that seems extreme, at least it is true that relationships are never easy, require patience and discipline and resolution, and are never just relationships of love, seen as 'free subjection to the will of another' (Zizioulas, 1985, p. 56) – which, indeed, may well express a form of masochism.

So how is the point that human persons are essentially social beings relevant to thinking about God? In God there are said to be just three persons (which may already seem rather restricted), and since they are all divine, what sort of relationship could they have to one another? Presumably they don't need pleasing or helping and are each perfectly happy and fulfilled already.

CHAPTER 28

An Ontology of the Personal?

Colin Gunton has argued strongly that the Trinity suggests an 'ontology of the personal' (Gunton, 1997, p. 195). The suggestion is that 'being' is not an impersonal and completely self-contained substance. Rather, it is essentially personal, and 'to be personal . . . is to be one whose being consists in relations of mutual communion with other persons' (Gunton, 1997, p. 195). I have argued that this is broadly true of human persons, though it hardly makes sense to speak of relations between entities which have no intrinsic properties at all. When I relate to other persons, I reveal to them something of my character and I receive from them some disclosure of their thoughts and feelings. Such thoughts and feelings have been shaped in turn by other persons, and the societies in which people live shape what they think and feel. But that does not mean that they have no thoughts and feelings of their own. They must have if they are to contribute to the changing social scene, and we know that some individuals contribute much more obviously and substantially than others. Human persons live in relation, but they also make their own unique contributions to the social web of relationships. They shape and are shaped by others. But a core of individuality is needed in order to receive, interpret, and creatively contribute to social relations. There cannot be just relations. There must be centres of interpretation and creativity which are the dynamic motors of social change.

This is true of human persons. But is it true of the source and sustainer of their being, of God? If the argument is that all beings must be personal, there would need to be some evidence for this, and it is hard to see what that evidence would be. For a start, there are many sub-personal beings in the universe. Electrons and atoms relate to one another and may all be interconnected at a physical level. These are relations, indeed, but they are not personal. They do not involve consciousness, value, or purpose. So an ontology of the personal cannot plausibly argue that all beings are really personal when many beings show no signs of it.

I think the claim is more likely to be that persons are the highest, most perfect sorts of being. And that is very problematic. Human persons, as we know them, are dependent, weak, fallible, quarrelsome, destructive, and short-lived. Most theologians have assumed that God, a perfect being, cannot be like that. Perhaps, like Richard Swinburne, we could posit a perfect person who knows everything, can do anything, and is necessarily good. This is stretching the idea of a 'person' considerably beyond our experience. What would such a perfect person have in common with us, and how could it be any sort of ideal or pattern for our lives? It would be even more unlike us than we are from a chimpanzee. It could not have our fears, our anxieties, our struggles and achievements, our rivalries and desires.

God does know and feel (is beatific) and has purposes, so God has mental properties, albeit very different from ours. That is a reason for saying that God is personal, if not a person. But God, as self-existent being, is infinitely more than that, and of that more there is little we can imagine. Is it true that a perfect being would necessarily have its being in relation to another? Gunton writes, 'three persons are for and from each other in their otherness. They thus confer particularity upon and receive it from one another'

(Gunton, 1997, p. 110). Each person gives its being to the others and receives its being from them. But a perfect being would surely be one which does not receive its being from any other. And while such a being might create others, it could not 'give its being' away. If it did so, it would have nothing left to give. It would be better to retain its being while generating other beings who could themselves experience goodness. The terminology of 'giving and receiving love' belongs to societies of needy and dependent beings who would be grateful for any help or encouragement they can get. A society of such beings would be good, but it would hardly be an example of absolute perfection.

The model of a social, mutually loving Trinity seems at first sight to be an attractive one. But the more it is explored in detail, the more it comes to seem radically unlike human societies. And therefore, human societies composed of very imperfect human persons may not be a good model for a supreme and perfect creator, or for the sort of love that such a creator may exhibit.

The divine society envisaged by social Trinitarians is very small and consists of just three persons, who are disembodied, morally perfect, incapable of development (since they are perfect), and free from suffering and from social hierarchy. Interestingly, both Gunton and Moltmann, who belong to non-Episcopal and relatively democratic churches, are sure that the divine society is totally democratic. It sounds very much as if they are projecting the Enlightenment values of democracy, equality, and fraternity upon God. There is nothing wrong with that, but they should not invert the historical order and suppose that these Enlightenment values issued from Trinitarian beliefs. The one-thousand-year gap between the formal announcement of orthodox Trinitarian beliefs and the rise of the Enlightenment suggests very strongly that they did not.

What sort of love could exist between the three perfect persons of the social Trinity? Love, in the ordinary human sense, involves caring for others in distress, helping them achieve their unique goods, creating and valuing such goods, developing together as different personalities, helping but leaving free, and cooperating when required. Difference is important to love, involving a sharing of differing perspectives and interests. All this depends on persons not being omnipotent and omniscient and wholly good, but sometimes being in need of help, needing to learn others' viewpoints, and learning patience, tolerance, empathy, and understanding.

What would love between three omnipotent, omniscient perfectly good beings be like? They might know each other completely and admire each other tremendously. But all the rich texture, the hurt, and the forbearance and forgiveness required by human love would be missing. They need no help, need to learn nothing, do not need to put up with another's foibles. What is the point of sharing when there is nothing new to learn, nothing one cannot already do, no possibility of development in self-sacrifice? What would one give up? What could you give an omnipotent person? What could you tell an omniscient person? Can you really value or love someone who is exactly the same as you? That might even seem strangely narcissistic, like loving your own reflection.

We develop a notion of human personhood by examination of human nature and of the sorts of activities that might develop and express it more fully. Such notions of personhood involve many complex factors, bound together in complex ways. Most of all, they involve both complementary and competitive relationships between persons with different specific capacities, between embodied beings who develop, mature, suffer, and die. Starting from there, we could begin to construct a thinner notion of personhood. We could progressively take away the body, then the fact of death, then differences of character and emotions. We would eventually be left with a very thin and abstract notion of person – perhaps a disembodied being who had knowledge, subjective apprehension, and intention. Once our concept of person was that thin, why would relationship to other persons be part of it? The very thin concept of a being who knows, feels, and intends need not logically make any reference to other similar beings. Such beings would have nothing to teach each other, no differing feelings to argue about, and no intentions which might conflict. They would lack almost everything that makes human persons so interesting. Is that notion of a person really a notion that would apply to a perfect God?

Too many strands of 'love' have been broken for this to count as the sort of love the New Testament ascribes to God. Real, thick love requires the existence of a being or beings who are truly 'other' than oneself, who have a real independence, whose experiences and capacities are different from one's own, and who are dependent and developing in many ways. If God is essentially love in this sense (a possibility I will explore in Part V), then some form of creation of others may indeed be a natural expression of the divine being. That does not mean that God must necessarily and always have created others to love. It means only that the expression of God's nature makes it natural that God will (not necessarily with-out beginning or intermission or end!) at some point create other persons in order to realise the divine nature as loving in relation to them.

Human persons are parts of societies wherein different capacities and personalities interact to produce particular sorts of pleasure or happiness. This is most obvious in the long period of dependency of infants upon adults, in the pleasures of sex, and in the feelings of loneliness that lack of social interaction can cause. Humans need to interact physically and socially in order to realise their distinctive capacities. To put it in a crude but telling way, you cannot play football on your own with any degree of satisfaction. Humans need other humans to realise their distinctive natures.

All this is true and important, and it provides a good reason, if a reason is sought, for why humans exist. They alone can produce the distinctive values of a dynamic, changing, and morally free social order – though the cost is that all human societies seem to collapse before the forces of envy, greed, and hatred, which is the negative side of human love. In fact, human love is something that has to be striven for against tendencies to control or to capitulate to others. It is a virtue, or complex of virtues – something that ought to be but usually is not. If you try to think of love between divine persons, you could not think of it as a virtue. Divine persons would have no selfish desires to overcome, and it is hard to think of them as needing the companionship of other divine persons – or as needing anything at all. Love within the Trinity does not seem to be anything at all like human love, so talk of what human persons must be like to enable human love to exist is hardly relevant at all to thinking of what is necessary for divine love to exist.

To summarise what I have said so far in Part IV, I have argued that there are severe problems with the view that persons are logically unique, are absolutely free, and are essentially relational. These are, I think, grossly exaggerated forms of characteristic features that human persons do possess. The concept of a human 'person' is indeed associated with notions of having a unique chain of experiences (even if this is not logical uniqueness). If uniqueness means 'not being a nature which can possibly be shared by others', then God the one and only creator of everything other than itself would be truly unique. But the divine persons, of which there are supposed to be three, would turn out not to be unique (precisely because there are three of them) and thus not divine persons as Zizioulas defines them.

Human persons are morally free (though this freedom is far from absolute). God, however, being perfect and incapable of doing evil, is not morally free, and the divine freedom is not absolute, since the essential divine existence and nature are necessary. Theologians have often argued that God is free not to create the universe. Yet social Trinitarians hold that God the Father necessarily generates the Son and the Spirit, which they do not hold to be a limit on divine freedom. Logically speaking, the necessary creation of some universe of finite persons would not impugn the divine freedom either, and it would leave the creation of this specific universe and the persons in it as a truly free divine act.

Human persons are essentially or properly social beings, and as such are involved in relationships of compassion and cooperation with other persons in a developing society, though this may not be a strictly necessary property. But social relationships entail the alterity or 'otherness' of the related persons, together with their social communion. Wherever this sort of communion exists, there must be a real otherness of being, whereas God is essentially one and undivided. Therefore if God is a relational being characterised by love, that relation must be to non-divine persons, and not a sort of secret self-love.

If there were divine persons, in the sense of subjects of consciousness, they would not have unique chains of experience unknown to the other persons, since they would all be omniscient. They would not have moral freedom, since they would already be perfect. And they would not need to care for or cooperate with other persons, since they would all be omnipotent. The more one analyses the notion of 'person', the less likely it seems that the Trinity can be conceived as three 'persons' in anything like the modern sense of 'person' as a conscious subject of willing and experience.

A good argument can be made for believing that the primordially ontological being will be personal in having knowledge and intention as well as being the first and only cause of all other beings. God might even be thought of as a person, if this is taken in a very 'thin' sense of being a unique, free, and relational substance. I have argued that to define God thus would be misleading, since God has other properties – such as self-existence, supreme beatitude, and being the sole cause of everything other than God – which do not belong to persons. But what does not seem necessary, or perhaps even possible, is to say that there are persons in the sense of three unique, free, and essentially related *hypostases* (substances) within God. It may be a conceptual advance to say that God is personal, conscious, creatively free, and capable of creating and relating to other personal beings, but this in itself provides no basis for speaking of God as Trinity.

CHAPTER 29

Intra-Trinitarian Love

The most powerful speculative argument for a three-consciousness view of the Trinity probably lies in the consideration that 'God is love' (1 John, 4, 8). The argument is that if God is essentially loving, then there must be someone for God to love. Richard Swinburne defines love partly as 'giving to the other what of one's own is good for him' (Swinburne, 1994, p. 177). God is omniscient and omnipotent, and if God is to give *fully* what is God's own, then God must create another omniscient, omnipotent being. There is a question about whether an omnipotent being can create another omnipotent being. Obviously not if 'omnipotence' means, or entails, that one has complete power over every other being so that one can create or destroy it at will. If God exists necessarily (that is, God exists whatever else may or may not exist and could not possibly fail to exist), then it may seem that no created being exists necessarily, since it could not exist without its creator. It may be, however, that God necessarily creates another being which, given the existence of God, could not fail to exist. That would entail that God could not destroy it. Yet their relation would be asymmetric, because God would be the cause of the created being, and it could not be the cause of God. The created being would be wholly dependent on the creating being, since the creator has given what is 'its own' to the created. The created being receives its power and knowledge from the uncreated being and could not ever oppose it or know anything that it did not know. This would not be an instance of mutual causation, so they would not be omnipotent in quite the same sense.

If these two beings acted, either one would have to make all the decisions and the other would have to agree, or there would have to be some mechanism which compelled them to agree in all decisions. Thus at least one of them would act under compulsion. The fact that it might always want to do what it was compelled to do is irrelevant to the fact that there would be a necessary limitation imposed by a being other than itself on what one of them could want. So one being would necessarily be dependent on the other, and at least one being would necessarily agree with what the other willed. This would mean that only one being could be absolutely omnipotent, though there could be two beings which necessarily existed and necessarily always agreed with each other. This might make one wonder what the advantage of having two such beings is. They always decide the same things, so the second being would seem to add nothing to the existence of the primary being.

It might be said that if it is good for one conscious being to exist, then it is even better for two conscious beings to exist. There would be two knowing and willing beings, even though one is a perfect clone of the other. It would be a loving act if the first being gave the good of happy existence to the second being. That good would otherwise not have existed. The second being would also enable the good of gratitude to exist, which otherwise would not have existed. Thus the existence of two beings would enable benevolence and gratitude to exist.

It should be noted, however, that the benevolence would cost nothing, and the gratitude would not be for a self-sacrificial gift, but rather for a process that occurred by necessity, not by an act of free choice that could have been otherwise. If you believe that an important part of being a person is the possession of libertarian freedom (freedom, in an exactly similar situation, to do one of alternative possibilities, not being constrained by another), this will make the relationship rather less than fully personal. The primary being would not have freely chosen to create, and the second being would not be grateful for a freely chosen and perhaps costly sacrifice but would, rather, be acknowledging a process that had to occur. Perhaps 'love' would not be an appropriate word for such a relationship after all.

Of course, if creation was an act of free choice, if it was costly (if, perhaps, it introduced suffering into an otherwise wholly beatific experience), and if the creature had some sort of independent freedom to which the creator might respond in creative ways, then something like personal love might be said to exist between creator and creation. But in this case we are talking about the creation of a non-divine being and not about the generation of other persons of the Trinity by God the Father. The question is whether love, in a fully personal sense, could exist within the Trinity in which the Son is generated by nature (necessarily) and not by will (freely and contingently). I think that a sort of love could exist in the being of God itself, but it would be significantly different from truly interpersonal love.

I have suggested that God might exhibit *philokalia*, love of the good. For it might be part of the perfection of God to know and understand good possible states, will their existence, and love (admire and appreciate) them for their own sake. This suggests a threefold nature of God as knowing, creating, and loving. But why should this being have to create another lover of what will be exactly the same goods?

It is true that creating another subject who knows and loves the good would be a good thing to do. It would increase the number of knowers of the good. But it is implausible to think that God has to do everything that is good; God does not, for example, have to create this universe, much less every possible good universe. God does not have to create every possible good there could ever be. Creating a specific universe is traditionally said to be 'an act of will' which could have been otherwise. Creating another perfect person would be an act of will too, as far as I can see. So it is something that it would be good for God to do but that God would not have to do.

CHAPTER 30

Infinite Gods

John Leslie has propounded what seems to me an interesting and powerful *reductio ad absurdum* of the argument that God has to create another 'person' within the divine being. He argues that there must be an infinite number of perfect Minds, since the more Minds there are, the more experiences of good there are (Leslie, 2001). If you think it is better to have many happy people than to have just one, you may be impressed by this argument. But it would seem to follow that the Father should generate an infinite number of Sons – and an infinite number of daughters too. The Holy Family must be infinitely large. Swinburne suggests that three is enough, but surely the more the better, and God must be as good as possible. An infinity of Gods (or of 'persons' in God, if you like) is better than just one, or just three, and there would be much more love to be given, received, and shared.

Most people instinctively feel there is something wrong with such an argument. But what is wrong with it? Leslie's argument depends upon the axiom that the more good things there are the better. He would then have to adopt the Leibnizian Rule that God must create the best of all possible worlds. So God must create an infinite number of good things, and an infinite number of other Gods. Or, to put it another way, as Leslie puts it, God must be a member of an infinitely large class of Gods. The argument seems valid – but only if you accept the Leibnizian Rule. That rule, however, can be denied in two main ways. First, there may not be such a thing as 'the best possible world'. There may just be an infinite number of different forms of goodness, and since there is no such thing as an actually infinite number of things, it is logically impossible for God to create all those goods. God will have to create a definite number of good things. Therefore God cannot create the 'best possible', since there is always at least one more thing that God could have created, whatever finite number of things God does create.

The second way in which the Leibnizian Rule can be denied is to say that God is not obliged to create anything, let alone the greatest number of good things. If God creates good things, that is good. If God creates more good things, that is better. But there is no 'best', and there is no obligation on God to create any good things at all, since God in the divine being is perfect anyway and it may be better to leave well alone.

John Leslie's argument actually introduces a new principle: that possible goodness is, in and of itself, 'a creative ethical requirement'. That is, if it is good for X to exist, then X ought to exist; therefore X will exist, simply because it ought to. This is what many people, I think rightly, find unconvincing. Many things that ought to exist do not exist (and many things that it seems ought not to exist do exist, such as horrendous evil or human sin). I would argue that if God, a supremely knowing and powerful being, exists necessarily, then if God acts intentionally, God will always act for the sake of good. That is because God will infallibly know what is good and will be able to realise it. A purely reasonable being will always act for a reason. And the only general reason for acting is that what one does is preferable, desirable, or, in a word, good.

This is indeed a sort of creative ethical requirement. But there is no requirement that every good thing should exist, and there is no requirement at all unless there is an actual being in whom that requirement can exist as a possible reason for acting. So I believe that John Leslie's argument stands in need of a theistic amendment. If God exists and is rational, there is a requirement that if God acts, God will act for the sake of good. But it is not an ethical requirement that God should create anything at all. In this way the argument that there should be an infinite number of persons in God fails. At the same time it looks as if an argument that God must necessarily generate another person (the Son) also fails. God does not necessarily generate another divine person. It might be good if God did, but God does not have to do so.

CHAPTER 31

Divine Love and Necessity

It could be argued, anyway, that God does not have to create another perfect person in order to be loving. The sort of love God could have for another perfect person would not differ substantially from the sort of love God already has for the good. Remember that the created perfect person would be qualitatively identical to God (Swinburne's argument, unlike that of Zizioulas, requires that the divine persons are qualitatively identical), except for the fact of being created. Love of such a person would not be *agape* love, costly love for those who could be in distress. It would be a thin sort of love, consisting simply of creating, loving (in the sense of acknowledging its goodness), and respecting (permitting, or at least necessarily coming to mutual agreement about whatever it does). There would, in a sense, be more good in existence. But there would be no real mutuality about the relationship of the two divine persons, since they would each know exactly the same things and would not need to help each other in any way (since both would be omniscient and omnipotent and never need help). Indeed, both would have to do exactly the same things, since they are said to differ in nothing 'except their relational properties' (Swinburne, 1994, p. 189). Their relationship would seem pretty vacuous.

Swinburne describes the divine persons as existing 'in mutual dependence and support' (Swinburne, 1994, p. 190). But this is a Pickwickian sense of dependence and support. They do not need or rely on each other for anything except, Swinburne suggests, in the logical sense that each person depends upon the other person not eliminating them and continuing to permit their existence. But there is no real sense of 'permitting' for two necessary beings. You do not need to permit what could not fail to be. So even that very thin sense of dependence and support fades away. The relationship seems more like mutual and compulsory toleration than like mutual love. Any argument for real love in God would necessitate the creation of truly other, and qualitatively different, persons. If God is free (especially if God is free in a libertarian sense), that would make the creation of other persons an act of will, not of essence. I conclude that a thinly loving God does not have to create another perfect person. An *agape* loving God would have to create some other persons, but they would be qualitatively different from God and would be chosen from among many alternatives. In any case, it is not clear that God necessarily has to love in an agapistic way, even though it might be natural for God to do so – and though Christians believe that God has in fact done so. Even then, the particular choice of which persons to create would be contingent, not necessary. And that would not properly describe the generation of the Son or Spirit by the Father.

Swinburne does not agree. He writes: 'Sharing with finite beings such as humans is not sharing all of one's nature and so is imperfect sharing' (Swinburne, 1994, p. 190). There is a necessity in God not just to create some other person but to create another person who has the greatest possible set of good-making properties – that is, who is qualitatively exactly like God, a divine clone. This is an ingenious and typically arresting suggestion. Certainly a relationship to a being of the same sort (say, a relationship between two human beings) is capable of being fuller and more meaningful than a relationship between two rather different sorts of beings (for instance, between a human and a gorilla). But in the case of omnipotent, omniscient, and purely spiritual beings, 'being of the same sort' seems to rule out differences of such things as temperament and taste. Then my intuition is that, if anything, there is a reason for not creating someone exactly like oneself. What would be lacking would be the possibility of diversity, of real help and support, and of real cooperation in doing things that individuals cannot do alone. A painless, effortless generation of an exact copy of oneself – while theoretically increasing the sum of good in existence – when you could also generate many different individuals who would genuinely introduce new sorts of values into existence seems regrettable. If, as Swinburne writes, 'there is something profoundly imperfect ... in a solitary divine individual' (Swinburne, 1994, p. 190), then one might retort that there is also something profoundly imperfect in an individual who produces an exact copy of himself and might well remain satisfied with that. God could cause a multitude of new and varied forms of persons, generating goods which otherwise could not have existed, and that would be much more worthwhile.

You may say that a really good God could create one or more perfect clones and also lots of finite persons. Perhaps that is so. But why should these clones be thought of as parts of God rather than as created copies? C. J. F. Williams, in a paper written in honour of Swinburne, writes: 'If love is God's nature, his love must have an object other than his creation ... to believe otherwise would be to make God dependent for his innermost activity on something that is not himself' (Williams, 1994, p. 238). Williams does not have an argument, like Swinburne, that there have to be three persons, no more and no less, in a loving relationship. But he assumes that love must be for another being and so depends upon there being something other than God, he assumes that God is essentially loving, and he assumes that God cannot be dependent on anything other than himself. Therefore the 'other being' must somehow exist within God. It seems to me just self-contradictory to say that there is 'real otherness' within a unitary and wholly simple God (as Williams, though not Swinburne, takes God to be). One cannot have both otherness within God and utter simplicity in the divine being.

The real objection to Williams' point, however, is this: suppose that God is essentially loving in an agapistic way (I am not convinced this is so, but suppose it is). Then it might be true that this entails that God creates some other object to love. But that object must be truly 'other' than God, not just 'part of' God. It does not follow, as Williams seems to think, that this makes God dependent on creation. It is God alone who wills that creation should exist as a condition of realising the divine nature as love. That is not a question of God being dependent on something completely independent of God. Nor does creation have to be co-eternal with God, if that is a problem. It is not the case that God has to be incessantly loving, only that God sometimes, or even often, creates an object to love (just as humans might essentially be thinking beings, but it does not follow that they never sleep). God might, as in some Hindu cosmologies, have periods of cosmic 'sleep' when God is not actually creating. In fact, the Genesis story of creation does speak of God 'resting' on the seventh day. It follows that God does not always have to be creating in order to essentially be a creator. Love may be God's nature, but even supposing that such love entails that God must create an object for God to love, it seems obvious that this object must be genuinely other than God and need not exist everlastingly but only for a finite time.

Suppose, then, that God creates a perfect clone. Would this not after all be an archangel rather than another truly divine person? Would the Arians not then be right in thinking of the eternal Son as the 'first creation', an exalted spiritual being but not one quantitively identical with God the creator of all? The usually quoted response to the Arians, that 'there was a time when the Son was not', misses the point. For the Son could easily be created by God and yet be co-eternal with God. Indeed, is it not obvious that the Son is 'the first-born of creation', since he is, as Son, in some sense 'begotten'? What can that mean if not created (i.e. brought into being)?

Swinburne's response is interesting. He distinguishes what he calls 'ontological necessity' from 'metaphysical necessity' (Swinburne, 1994, p. 118). Something that is ontologically necessary is something that is everlasting and has, and can have, no cause at all. Something that is metaphysically necessary is something that is everlasting and only has an uncaused cause which causes it inevitably. He then says that if the Son was ontologically necessary, then a generated Son, caused by the Father, could not be divine. But if the Son is metaphysically necessary, it can inevitably and everlastingly be caused by the Father and be divine. So whether the Son is divine or not depends upon whether the generation of the Son is or is not inevitably caused by an uncaused being.

This seems to me a very arbitrary proposal. It suggests that if the Spirit is caused by both Father and Son, as Swinburne thinks it is, then the Spirit is not divine. For though the generation of the Spirit might be inevitable, it is partly generated (for Swinburne) by the Son, who is not uncaused. So the Spirit fails the test for being metaphysically necessary. It also suggests that the only thing that makes the 'second person' divine, as opposed to being an archangel clone of God, is that it is everlastingly and necessarily caused by God the Father. This is a very fine distinction to make between a divine person and an everlasting archangel with precisely the same properties as a divine person (omniscience and omnipotence) which God did not have to create but which God could freely will to create.

Questions about what is and what is not necessary to God are very hard, almost certainly impossible, for humans to answer. The consequence is that it is almost impossible for us to tell whether the second person is divine or not on Swinburne's criteria. That does seem rather odd. It may lead one to suspect that the relation between Father and Son within the Trinity must be closer than, and thus different from, the relation between an uncreated person and an identical created (or 'generated') person. There must be a clearer distinction between creation and 'generation' – one that will not lead one to say that the 'generated' Son is a different conscious being from the Father.

There are, of course, three persons in the Trinity. The argument from divine love so far only gets us to two persons – though, as I have pointed out, I do not see why it may not equally plausibly get us to a much larger number of identical persons. That would be even better than two, so why should that not be necessary too? I think Swinburne's only argument here is one of economy: there should be as few entities as possible, compatibly with God's being essentially loving. That is hardly consistent with his point that 'goodness is essentially diffusive' (Swinburne, 1994, p. 190). It is not very generous just to create one perfect person, the minimum possible, when one could create so many more.

However, Swinburne tries to get to three persons, again just by reasoning alone. He does so by introducing a new stipulation about love, which is influenced by Richard of St. Victor's claim that love must be given, received, and shared with another: 'love must share and love must co-operate in sharing' (Swinburne, 1994, p. 178). That may very well be true with finite persons such as human beings. For two people to share their love with each other but exclude everyone else from it would be a very restricted sort of love. But the analogy begins to look weak when it turns out that shared divine love will only include one other person. A one-child family among humans is not always the best expression of human love. Why should it be the best expression of divine love?

Why, in any case, should two identical divine persons 'co-operate' in creating a third identical divine person? They could each, as omnipotent, do it on their own. They are bound to agree in everything they do anyway. The best one can say is that both agree to create a third companion. Again, it would no doubt be good to do so. But is it necessary that they should create one and only one? How do we know that it is necessary for them to do that? Is the third really a companion? The first two do not teach the Spirit or guide its development – it has no development. They do not rejoice in its triumphs and sympathise with its mistakes – it has no triumphs, since everything is easy for omnipotence. And it makes no mistakes, since an omniscient being can never be in error. Like the two-divine-person relation, a three-divine-person relation would lack almost everything that is important about human love and about what it is for anyone to share their love with others. It does not matter to the divine persons how many divine persons there are, and it makes a minimal difference to them, which is perhaps why they opt for as few persons as possible.

Christians notoriously disagree about whether the Spirit is generated from only the Father (as the Orthodox think) or from the Father and the Son together (as Swinburne thinks, even though he is Orthodox). That suggests that the argument is not as a priori as all that and that other factors (probably Biblically based, though it is odd that there is such disagreement about what is in the Bible) are doing all the real work.

Swinburne ends his chapter on the Trinity by saying: 'the most probable kind of God is such that inevitably he becomes tripersonal' (Swinburne, 1994, p. 191). It is odd that no other religion, and no system of natural theology, has thought of that. It is odd that any human being, by purely rational argument without appeal to revelation, should presume to say what is inevitable for God. And it is odd to subject the divine being to rules of probability (whether Bayesian or not) which only function where statistical information is available and can at least be roughly quantified – which seems not to be the case with God. Despite the psychological appeal and intellectual rigour of Swinburne's arguments on this point, they do seem Procrustean; the arguments are beautifully shaped to fit facts which are believed on quite other grounds, and the arguments otherwise do not seem at all convincing.

What seems to be happening is that a set of analogies drawn from human love – which may work to some extent when we are considering God's love in relation to human beings – is being projected onto God and considered out of relation to anything but God. The whole point, however, of the argument from God's love to God's relational and passionate nature is to escape from Hellenistic philosophical arguments about God's self-sufficiency and impassibility and take more seriously Biblical remarks about God's relation to the prophets and saints. These remarks refrain from saying much about God considered apart from all relationships and affective responses to the actions of human beings. The prophet Isaiah says, 'To whom then will you liken God, or what likeness compare with him? . . . His understanding is unsearchable' (Isaiah 40, 18, and 28). If the *ousia*, the immanent being of God, is beyond human comprehension, perhaps humans should be very wary of applying a priori arguments to discover its precise nature.

CHAPTER 32

Love and Alterity

No discussion of social Trinitarianism would be complete without reference to the work of Jurgen Moltmann, who is the best-known exponent of an extreme form of what he himself terms a 'social' view. In the course of his exposition, he, like Swinburne, develops a powerful analysis of what divine love must be. The analysis is profound, but in the end I think it fails to support social Trinitarianism. Moltmann argues that a being which needs nothing outside itself is somehow morally inferior, self-satisfied, and inward-looking. Aristotle's God, who loves himself as the best of all things, would seem, from this point of view, incurably egotistical and self-centred. But a desire is only selfish if it puts one's own desires before those of others. Where there are no others, selfishness logically cannot exist.

There could be, perhaps, a sort of analogue of selfishness if God preferred 'lower goods' to 'higher goods', or 'short-term pleasures' to 'long-term pleasures'. But God, being perfectly wise, knowing, and powerful, not logically capable of being tempted by sensual pleasures, and not being short of time, has no reason to choose lower-quality or shorter-term goods. God will always choose the objectively good for its own sake. Since the good is part of the divine reality, that could be seen as a sort of self-love, I suppose. But in this case the 'self' would not be opposed to the good. It would not even be capable of being opposed to the good. It would be identical with the good, as both 'willed' and 'loved' by the self.

I have suggested that it makes sense to say that God knows, wills, and loves the supreme good, and in doing so enjoys supreme beatitude. This is a form of threefoldness in God, and it may be the ontological basis of God's threefold being in relation to creation. But it does not entail that God must be constituted by three persons. If there were three persons in God, each divine person would love the good and all would love the same good. None would be selfish, and none, being omnipotent, would need the others. So why should the fact that God is loving require that there be three distinct subjects of consciousness within God?

A loving being, Moltmann says, needs to centre its being on something other than itself to 'enter into other being' and 'give itself for other being' (Moltmann, 1981, p. 57). Where there are other beings who could be benefitted by your self-giving and who have personal experiences to share with others, this may be true. Even in such a case, there is reason to be suspicious of talk of 'total self-giving'. Moltmann is aware of this and talks of 'self-communication of the good without self-renunciation', but there is a danger in speaking of a complete submission of the will to another. Women and slaves are only too aware of the way in which such a doctrine has been used for the domination of one gender or class by others on allegedly moral grounds. Mutual love is something that both gives well-being to and receives it from another, and it seems much healthier than a slavish submission of oneself to the wishes of another.

But in the case of divine persons, no person would benefit by the self-giving of another, since each person is supremely happy in love of the good anyway. And no person has private experiences to share with another, since all divine persons know all there is to be known. There is, to put it bluntly, no point in a divine person giving itself to another divine person, since they both already possess everything that is worthwhile. Loving companionship, compassion, and cooperation are great and distinctive human virtues. It might be worth creating a universe in which they could exist. If such a universe does exist, since persons in it would be finite, dependent, needy, and perhaps suffering and lonely, it would certainly be good for God to love them, to make a loving divine presence known to them, to care for their welfare, and to cooperate with them for good. In that sense, it would be good for a perfect God to love created persons in a fully compassionate and cooperative sense.

Moltmann holds that God necessarily creates a universe containing other persons and that God necessarily loves other (created) persons, since it is part of the essential nature to love. That is a strong argument for the necessity of the creation of some persons who are other than God. But how could it be an argument for the creation of 'other' divine persons – persons who are not really other than God at all?

The argument that it is necessary for a loving God to create other persons who can be loved fails to support a doctrine of the Trinity. The statement that God is necessarily loving implies only that the one and only God must create other, non-divine persons to be objects of the divine love. Social Trinitarians, however, often argue that unless God the Father first generated divine persons to love in eternity, even before or apart from any creation, God would not really be able to love created persons. This seems to be a complete non sequitur, and I can see no reason to think it is true. It is in fact a relic of the Aristotelian tradition that God must be completely perfect in the divine being alone, without any other being. Yet this is just what Moltmann is denying, in holding that love requires true otherness. Far from supporting a social view of the Trinity, Moltmann's argument at this point seems more compatible with altogether denying the need for a Trinity.

Colin Gunton argues that 'It is because God is a communion of love prior to and in independence of the creation that he can enable the creation to be itself' (Gunton, 1997, p. xviii). This implies that a Unitarian God could not 'enable creation to be itself', and Gunton goes on to say, 'The logic of all Unitarian thought . . . brings God and the creation too closely together' (Gunton, 1997, p. 129) and leads to pantheism. This seems to be very obviously false. Jewish and Muslim monotheists are usually not pantheists, and the question of whether the cosmos is part of God's being is an entirely distinct question from that of whether God is threefold. I suspect that what Gunton has in mind is that a Unitarian God might have to be a God who unilaterally determines everything that happens, thus allowing no real creative freedom to creatures. I do not think that is so. But there is something in the point that a God who permits real 'otherness' and autonomy in creatures, and who is truly loving, might have to act to guide and unite creatures to the divine. This would be a creative, relational, responsive, and dynamic God rather than an unchanging and impassible source of being. It makes sense to think that this gives a threefold structure to God, as creator, cooperator, and integrator of otherness into the divine life – though Unitarians, Jews, and Muslims would not put it exactly like this. But in any case this is a Trinity-in-relation-to-creation, an economic Trinity, which does not necessarily transfer to the concept of God *in se*. Also, ironically, this sort of Trinity, which gives to all creation a share in the nature of God, is more like pantheism than a strict Jewish or Muslim view that God always remains apart from creatures who can have no real share in the divine nature. Presumably, Christians would think there is nothing wrong with this sort of pantheism.

Indeed, if you wanted to invent an argument in this arcane area, a better argument might be that if God was (as God is not) a perfect communion of love without creation, then God would have no need of creation at all – and of course that is a traditional Christian view. It is only if God is a being who can will to express the divine nature by being concerned for others who need such concern that God has reason to create a universe as an 'other' which God can love. In short, there is no compelling argument that, in order to have a universe of free persons, its creator must consist of three cooperating consciousnesses. A fully monotheistic God can create many free persons and relate to them in compassion and coopera-tion if God wishes to do so. I would think this is exactly what Christians believe that God does. But this in itself does not entail that God is some sort of society. It does not even entail (though it is consistent with the view) that God is Trinitarian.

CHAPTER 33

Trinity versus Monotheism

Moltmann has other arguments for social Trinitarianism too. His most provocative is his condemnation of monotheism as theologically, morally, and politically harmful. It is certainly a startling thought that monotheism is opposed to Trinitarian theism, but it is a thought he repeats a number of times.

Moltmann frequently says that belief in one God leads to belief in one all-determining ruler, which leads to hierarchical, patriarchal, and dictatorial views in politics and church organisation, and is opposed to true Christian belief in the equal freedom of all, where a true concern for and service of others will mark a truly democratic and humane society. 'Monotheism', he writes, 'was and is the religion of patriarchy' (Moltmann, 1981, p. 165). But if we believe in a Trinitarian God, in which belief no person will be superior to another and where all give themselves in love to the others, we will, he claims, have a much better model for human social relations.

The move from theological doctrine to political programme seems much too quick. Is there any reason to think that belief in one knowing/acting divine subject has any logical connection at all with belief that there should be one dictator with unlimited powers in human societies? The one divine subject might well issue orders that, since God is the only source of all authority, no human being is to set themselves in absolute authority over others. Perhaps, such a God may say, humans are so fallible and quarrelsome that none of them should ever claim supreme authority to interpret the will of God. All should have humility before the mystery of God, and it may be forbidden for anyone to claim to stand in the place of God and assume absolute authority over other 'miserable worms'. I am not asserting that God does say that, though there are certainly forms of Islam that do. I just cannot see any logically valid way to infer from 'There is only one God' that 'There should be only one absolute ruler in human societies'.

In any case, if you were looking for a logical link between religious beliefs and political organisations, you might think that radical poly-theists were more likely to be democratic than Trinitarians. After all, three divine persons is a rather small number, and a Gang of Three absolute rulers is not much better than one absolute ruler. What we would want is no rulers at all, or a group of more-or-less democratic rulers, such as the Olympian gods, perhaps. Better still, Buddhists, with no supreme God at all, should have much the most democratic system. But that is not in itself a strong argument for Buddhism.

If there is no logical connection between monotheism and dicta-torship, could Moltmann's claim be an empirical one that, while there is no real reason for it, monotheists in fact tend to support dictator-ships whereas Trinitarians do not? The problem is that most human societies tend to support dictatorships from time to time, whatever they think about God. It is certainly true that some of the most Trinitarian societies in history – for example, the Eastern Orthodox churches – have supported very tyrannical governments. The Byzantine Empire is not a very good example of a liberal and democratic system, though it was strongly Trinitarian. And I sup-pose Unitarians would be very democratic and free-thinking if there were enough of them to make a difference.

In fact I think there is no reason to support Moltmann's claim about monotheism and political theology at all. He is, of course, a notable supporter of liberation theology and has argued that Christian faith should engage in political action for giving everyone, and especially the poor and disadvantaged, social and economic rights and freedoms. This involves the claim that all human persons should be concerned for others, compassionate, and loving – and that they should work to put social structures in place that would make that more feasible. It also involves the claim that God commands love and compassion on the part of believers. I think it is true that the example of Jesus as the human manifestation of a loving, compassionate God would be very important in supporting such a view. But that is true whatever theory one has about the Trinity. Whether you have a three-consciousness view or a one-consciousness view of God, you can believe that Jesus shows the nature of God as loving and compassionate. Unitarians too can quite coherently hold that 'God is love', meaning that God loves the good and loves creation and loves particular persons.

CHAPTER 34

The Passion of Christ

Moltmann's 'social' doctrine of the Trinity really begins, however, from the passion of Christ and with the insistence that this manifests the suffering of God. God is passionate love and is revealed by Christ's passion to be one who is intimately affected by the suffering of others – one who suffers with others. This is a powerful argument, though it is not an argument which could apply to the relationship of diverse persons within the Trinity. This is because it would seem that the Trinitarian persons, if there were no created world, would have no reason to suffer, and so there is no place for compassion among the divine persons.

Moltmann denies this, for he says, 'The love with which God . . . loves the world is no different from the love he himself is in eternity' (Moltmann, 1981, p. 59). God's eternal intra-Trinitarian love is the same as God's love for the world. Since God's love for the world, in all its suffering, involves empathetic suffering, then God's eternal love 'contains the pain of the negative' (Moltmann, 1981, p. 57). There is a sort of 'contradiction' or 'rift' within the divine being, even in eternity. It is hard to see why this should be so if there is no world of sufferers in existence and if the divine persons do not suffer themselves.

However, Moltmann's general argument entails that God must create the world: 'God "needs" the world and man' (Moltmann, 1981, p. 58), because love seeks fellowship and desires response. It is not enough for God to love beings exactly like God; there must also be an unlike other to love. Moreover, 'creation means . . . self-humiliation' (Moltmann, 1981, p. 59). Creation itself entails suffering, in which God must share. Though he says that immanent and economic Trinities are identical, Moltmann makes this true by making creation, suffering, and sin to be necessary objects of divine love. This makes such love a sharing in suffering and a bearing of the cost of sin. There is no eternal Trinity in the sense of a Trinity without and apart from creation. There is only the Trinity as it is necessarily involved in going out from itself into creation and 'suffering love'. But if there is no eternal Trinity other than the Trinity involved in creation and suffering, then there is no possibility of an intra-Trinitarian love in addition to the extra-Trinitarian love that is the essential character of God. Moltmann says, 'Love cannot be consummated by a solitary subject' (Moltmann, 1981, p. 57). Moreover, God 'expects and needs love' (Moltmann, 1981, p. 99). God gives himself in love; but he also needs to have love returned, to be changed by being loved by the other. The natural conclusion is that the creation of another person or persons is necessary to the being of God as love and that the existence and actions of other persons will change the being of God.

It may seem that divine love could be realised within the Trinity itself, and Moltmann sometimes suggests that it is. This, however, is very problematic for Moltmann. It should not be possible for him to speak of God apart from any creation. 'The notion of an immanent Trinity in which God is simply by himself . . . brings an arbitrary element into the concept of God', he says (Moltmann, 1981, p. 151). 'The God who loves the world does not correspond to the God who suffices for himself.' He writes that he favours a form of panentheism for which all creation is, or is eventually to be, included within God. God is 'the God who unites others with himself' (Moltmann, 1981, p. 150), and the unity of the divine being is a unity which is 'communicable, open, inviting', not closed and exclusive. One reason Moltmann finds it unhelpful to speak of God as a substance is that, according to him, substances are not open. They are complete and self-enclosed, he thinks. God, on the other hand, has a history that includes humans, and his unity is 'unitedness' or the fellowship of persons rather than aseity.

He particularly dislikes the idea of aseity. 'Rahner's reinterpretation of the doctrine of the Trinity', he writes, 'ends in the mystic solitariness of God. It obscures the history of the Father, the Son, and the Spirit to which the Bible testifies, by making this the external illustration of that inner experience [of God]. Is there really any 'greater danger' than this 'modalism'?' (Moltmann, 1981, p. 148). It is rather odd that he castigates Rahner in this way, since he accepts Rahner's well-known suggestion that the economic Trinity is identical with the immanent Trinity. I cannot see that in Rahner there is any 'mystic solitariness', or any hidden noumenal reality, behind the Trinitarian appearances. God is Trinitarian in the essential divine nature – and that is just what Moltmann thinks too, although that 'essential divine nature' is taken by Moltmann to be a society of three.

Moltmann's objection seems to be that, in the end, Rahner thinks that God is one substance, which means that God is completely self-enclosed from, unrelated to, and unchanged by what happens in the world. It is true that many theologians have believed that. But that belief does not follow from the idea that God is a substance (or an 'absolute subject', possessing knowledge and will, a concept to which Moltmann also objects). As William Alston points out, primary substances for Aristotle are not completely self-enclosed, unrelated, or unchanging. Ordinary substances, such as 'this man' or 'this dog', are continually changing in their properties and relate in many ways to other substances. There is no reason at all why God should not be a substance, an individual bearer of properties, which is also a subject, having the properties of consciousness, knowledge, and will, and which is essentially related to other substances in a process of continual change. Indeed, on Moltmann's own view, each divine person is a distinct person and subject (Moltmann, 1981, p. 140). Presumably these subjects are individual substances, in Aristotle's sense, and yet they are essentially open and related. So there is no logical reason for denying that God could be one open and related substance and subject. Given the impossibility, according to Moltmann, of speaking of an immanent God apart from creation and the necessity of creating a world of other finite persons, this does not really sound like a defence of a social Trinity.

CHAPTER 35

God and Abandonment

Moltmann speaks of God necessarily creating a world which contains evil, chaos, and the threat of non-being. 'When we say "God is love", then we mean that he is in eternity ... a process which contains the whole pain of the negative in itself. God loves the world with the very same love which he himself is in eternity' (Moltmann, 1981, p. 57). So the intra-Trinitarian relations already (from eternity) contain pain. God is self-communicating, self-limiting, suffering, and redemptive love.

I find this a moving and powerful exposition of the New Testament Gospel of the unlimited, creative, and redemptive love of God. But it does not entail that these properties belong to God *in se*, even without any creation. For if God's love creates a world of 'unlike' persons to receive and return divine love, that in itself enables God's nature as agapistic love to be fully realised. There is no need to postulate a strange sort of internal opposition and battle between suffering and goodness within the being of God.

Is it satisfactory, anyway, to see the divine persons as distinct subjects in fellowship? Moltmann, as previously noted, refers to Biblical texts which stress that the Father 'sends' the Son, the Son refers to 'God' (the Father) as another, and the Spirit is sent by the Father at the request of the Son. That can certainly sound like three distinct subjects of experience and action. But there is a major problem, and it lies at the heart of Moltmann's concern with the crucified God. John's Gospel says, 'God so loved the world that he gave his only Son . . . ' (John 3, 16). But it does not seem in keeping with suffering love for a Father to send his own Son to be crucified. Surely it must be God who is crucified for human sin, not just one of three divine persons. Of course God is crucified in the human person of Jesus, and the great theological tradition has held that the divine nature did not suffer, though the human nature of Jesus did. Moltmann is among many more-recent theologians who protest that the divine nature must suffer if God really does love and empathise with creatures. But then he insists that only one divine person suffers the pain of the cross. The Father suffers the pain of watching his Son die, and the Son suffers the pain of abandonment by his Father. Presumably the Spirit suffers in empathy with both. There is suffering in God, but three different types of suffering – and this leaves an uncomfortable feeling that a really loving Father would not send his Son to suffer.

It is for this reason that Moltmann holds that we can only talk of divine suffering if there are three persons in God; 'in monotheism it is impossible' (Moltmann, 1981, p. 25), he writes. But why should a monotheist not consistently hold that God is capable of suffering? And why should the idea of divine suffering imply that there are different sorts of suffering, and therefore different persons in God? In fact, there are great difficulties with Moltmann's theory that the divine persons experience different sorts of suffering. If we introduce a doctrine of total omniscience, then of course each person will experience what the others experience. This means that both Father and Spirit will experience Jesus' Passion and death on the cross. They will not experience it as their own, but they will experience it with full intensity and affective force, by a total empathy that cannot be paralleled in human experience. This seems to mean on Moltmann's account that the Father must fully experience what it is like to be abandoned by the Father, and the Son must fully experience what it is like to abandon one's own Son to a cruel death. Yet it seems impossible for even a divine person to feel simultaneously what it is like to be abandoned and to abandon and to know (as the Spirit does) that such abandonment is not final. If the Son, as omniscient, experienced all these things, then the Son could not truly have felt abandoned, for the Son would also have known the Father's grief and the Spirit's power.

It is possible that the human consciousness of Jesus could have felt the absence of God's sustaining presence. Although the Spirit filled the life of Jesus, so that throughout his life he had a vivid sense of God's presence and of inspiration by divine wisdom, it is possible that he lost this sense on the cross, that he experienced, as many saints do, a 'dark night of the soul'. Thereby Jesus could truly enter into the sense of anguish and solitude that marks so many human lives that are estranged from God. He could have experienced what it is like to be separated from God – even though he was never actually abandoned by God.

In that sense we might say that Jesus on the cross did feel the agony of suffering and abandonment by his followers, as well as a sense of the absence of the divine presence. But, as the eternal Son, he never could have been abandoned by the Father, and he never could have felt abandonment by his Father. In other words, the Son could not have experienced total abandonment by God – just as no divine person could ever have experienced the pleasure of a torturer hard at work or of a serial rapist. They would know what such an experience was like, but they would at the same time have condemned it and distanced themselves from it. So the Son could have experienced what being forsaken was like – as could the Father and the Spirit – but he could not (if omniscience exists) have believed that he really was abandoned, and in that sense the experience would have been mitigated, even though the suffering would have been real and, from a human point of view, agonising.

Many modern theologians feel that we want more from a loving God than the rather abstract knowledge that Jesus suffers. We want God to feel that suffering in the divine being itself. If we sympathise with that thought, we might well want more from a loving Father than grief at the suffering of his Son. We want Father and Spirit to feel that suffering too. In other words, we want there to be one experience of suffering, even if felt in different particular forms. The Father does not send someone else to suffer without feeling that suffering intensely and without mitigating that suffering by infusing a sense of compassion and hope. Complete omniscience suggests that there is one experience, shared in different particular modes of subsistence, rather than three separate subjects of private experience.

Presumably Moltmann must hold that such complete omniscience breaks down at least at the crucifixion; otherwise there would be no sense of 'abandonment by the divine' within the divine being itself. So he must think that the divine persons can at times oppose or misunderstand one another: 'God is forsaken by God' (Moltmann, 1981, p. 80). Even worse, 'the Father cast him [the Son] off and cursed him (Moltmann, 1981, p. 81). That would be a good reason for stressing real distinctness, otherness, and difference within God. On the other hand, it seems to entail an ontological monstrosity, a pathological breakdown in the inner life of God. If such a thing could occur, there would no longer be a unity of will and knowledge in God, and the unity of God would break apart into an overt polytheism in which different divine beings could curse one another and misunderstand one another (the Son thinking the Father has abandoned him when God never could). At this point, the social Trinity collapses into polytheism and is only saved from disintegration by the controlling monarchy of the Father, who thereby becomes the only true God.

Not all theologians accept my assessment. Hans Urs von Balthasar is perhaps the best-known modern theologian who argues in favour of 'an absolute infinite distance' between Father and Son, 'a unique and incomprehensible 'separation' of God from himself'' (von Balthasar, 1994, IV, pp. 323–325). Von Balthasar thinks of this internal separation of divine persons as belonging to the immanent Trinity in itself, not just to the historical event of the cross. However emotionally powerful this presentation of an experiencing of complete abandonment and its overcoming within the life of God may be, it seems to me like a projection onto an unknown (the inner life of God) of events which belong properly only to history and to the involvement of God with a diverse and estranged creation. And it introduces a contradiction into the foundational notion of God as of supreme value. The contradiction is only intensified by the thought that the Father on the one hand gives everything without reserve to the Son and on the other hand places an infinite distance between the Son and himself. It is hard to see how both these things can be the case. Von Balthasar's account of the Trinity is a social Trinitarian account inasmuch as it makes the divine persons as different from one another as they could possibly be, even though it says that everything is given freely and fully from the Father to the Son.

What both von Balthasar and Moltmann do powerfully argue for is the self-giving relation of God to creation, the involvement of God in the suffering of the world, and the divine institution of a historical process which culminates in the final inclusion of creation within the being of God. These are creative and imaginative insights, but, except by a purely speculative projection of the economic Trinity into the inner being of God *in se*, they do not entail the idea that God is a (rather small) society.

I think that they do suggest, if not entail, that God not only creates the universe, but also expresses the divine being within the universe and interacts in a real way with created reality to unite it to the divine. Despite Moltmann's defence of a social Trinity, these acts of God can adequately be thought of as three different modes of subsistence – creative, self-communicative, and unitive – of one unitary will and knowledge. The same God acts in three ways and therefore manifests the same agency in three different forms, instantiations, or loci of action. And that is not a social doctrine of the Trinity at all. But it does suggest that the Trinitarian God has a real history with the created world and a real relationship to created persons, which involves God in both the suffering and the final joy of the creative process. Those are insights which make the idea of the triune God both coherent and illuminating.

PART V

The Cosmic Trinity

CHAPTER 36

The Doctrine of *Perichoresis*

In Part IV I considered some main arguments in recent theology that have been offered in support of a 'social' view of the Trinity. This view holds that there are three persons in God in the sense of distinct centres of consciousness and will. It is obviously of great importance to decide what a 'person' in this sense is. First of all I examined some claims that have been made about the nature of persons, namely that persons are ontologically prior to substances. On this view, they do not evolve from unconscious substances and cannot be completely analysed in terms of unconscious substances or general 'natures' but in fact form the ultimate and irreducible sources of all being. They are absolutely free in that they are not bound by some impersonal necessity but determine their own beings. And they are essentially relational and cannot exist in isolation but have their being in relation to other persons in a communion of being. I made the following comments about these claims: persons should not simply be contrasted with substances, since they are themselves sentient, intelligent, and freely acting substances. They possess important creative freedom, but that freedom is not absolute, since even the ultimate being of God has a necessary nature, one part of which is precisely to possess the capacity of free creative choice. And although relation to others is a property that often fulfils personal being, persons are more than the set of relationships in which they are involved, and they have an important core of unique personal experience and self-unfolding action.

It does not seem that God, the one and only creator of the universe, either is a person or consists of three persons in these senses. God is less limited and dependent than persons, though God possesses personal properties. In particular, it does not seem to be true that if God were personal, God could not be a substance (a completely self-existent being), could not have a necessary nature, and would have to consist of more than one person. So there is not an argument for a social Trinity here, though to insist that God is freely creative and would only realise the divine nature as fully personal by relating to other (presumably created) persons is an interesting revision of some traditional Christian ideas of God.

I proceeded to examine what I consider to be the strongest argument for a social Trinity – the argument that if 'God is love', there must be a plurality of loving persons in God. I urged that there is a good argument here for God's creation of a world of finite persons to whom God can relate in love but that the idea of 'parts' of God loving each other utilises a very restricted and almost vacuous idea of love. I am not convinced that God can only realise the divine nature by creating a universe so that creation becomes necessary to God being what God is. But I do accept that God has actually expressed the divine being as agapistic love by the creation of finite persons. I think this must be seen as a natural and proper expression of the divine nature, but I regard it as a step too far to say that this is what God had to do and that there is no other way in which God could fully be God. Yet even if some creation was necessary to God, that would not make God dependent upon something other than God. God would still be the creator of everything other than God, and creation would then be an essential divine property rather than, as I think it is, a contingent and gratuitous act of divine grace.

Finally, I examined the claim that God could not share in the suffering of the world unless there was more than one person in God, indeed a sort of 'rift' or opposition within the being of God. Rejecting this idea as incoherent, I concluded that the idea of a social Trinity not only threatens belief in one supreme God, but cannot be supported by argument and undermines the strongest reason for creation – namely that the perfection of the divine being is expressed uniquely and graciously in the relationship and responsiveness to created beings that only a communion of love can provide.

Here in Part V I will examine the social view as it is presented in the work of some modern theologians in the analytical tradition and argue that they qualify the view to such an extent that it becomes virtually indistinguishable from a sophisticated one-consciousness view. This will involve a fuller analysis of the concept of *perichoresis*, to which some of these theologians appeal, in particular of whether or in what way the persons of the Trinity have different experiences and to what extent they can be said to have separate wills. I will suggest that the social view arises from a dubious projection of the economic Trinity onto the immanent Trinity and that a one-consciousness view is able to distinguish the economic from the immanent Trinity more clearly without falling into modalism. I will conclude with a positive summary of the final account of the Trinity I have given, which I call 'cosmic' because it conceives of God in relation to a hugely expanded cosmos and not just to humans on this planet.

The influential American philosophers William Alston and Cornelius Plantinga separately defend the view that the Trinity is coherently construable as three persons (or substances, in Aristotle's sense of primary substance, as individual bearers of properties) in one substance (in Aristotle's sense of secondary substance, essential nature). On this view there are three individual substances of a rational nature (to use Boethius' definition of 'person', which Alston quotes) all having the same essential divine nature (presumably including omniscience, omnipotence, and perfect goodness).

The philosophers see, however, that this is awkwardly like having three divine beings or gods. Accordingly, they add the condition that the three persons must be inseparable co-actors in every divine action – Alston quotes Gregory of Nyssa as saying, 'Every operation has its origin from the Father, and proceeds through the Son, and is perfected in the Holy Spirit' (Alston, 1999, p. 192). Although neither author provides a detailed analysis of this inseparability, there seem to be three main features of it. First, no divine person can act separately or on its own initiative. All three persons cooperate in every action; no divine act is performed by one person alone. Second, each person complements the others, contributing one element of each divine action without which the action would not be complete. Third, the persons exhibit *perichoresis*. They do not just agree; they 'interpenetrate', or dwell in one another. They exhibit what John of Damascus calls 'an identity of *ousia*, operation, and will' (Alston, 1999, p. 192). That, John stresses, is not just similarity; it is identity.

This, they think, is sufficient to assure the identity of one divine substance. Indeed it is, but does the three-consciousness view now differ in any way from the view it opposes, that God is one personal being, one subject of consciousness, knowledge, and will, not three? If three persons necessarily and inseparably cooperate in every action, there must be something that necessitates and guarantees this cooperation. Since there is not a 'fourth super-person' who brings that about, some (Zizioulas, for example) suggest that the Father is the ultimate and only source of the being and nature of the other divine persons. Son and Spirit do not have wholly independent wills which may differ from that of the Father; they necessarily will what the Father wills. This, however, suggests a difference between the Father and the other two persons, and suggests that on this view only the Father is really a wholly ungenerated and independently intentional agent. Being self-existent and the cause of everything other than himself, the Father is in a position to know that he is omniscient, that there exists nothing that he does not know. The generated persons are not in such a position, for they have to rely on the trustworthiness of the Father's mental content to be sure that they are omniscient! It sounds as if only the Father is fully God.

The Father generates another two divine persons. But why only two? Brian Leftow suggests that the Father could generate millions of persons or 'gods'. However, twelve – a good number for a society, sociologists tell us – would seem reasonable. Then what would the difference be between the Greek Olympian gods and the Trinity? The main thing wrong with pagan polytheism, Leftow writes, might have been that it 'preached a few too many divine beings, and did not know how alike, akin, and in accord all divine beings truly are' (Leftow, 1999, p. 230).

The problem goes even deeper. If *every* act of God is supposed to be an act of the three persons acting together, then how can it be that the Father alone generates the Son and the Spirit? There will be at least one generative act that is not performed by the Trinity as a whole. This does, as Leftow also argues, seem to privilege the Father as superior in a clear way to Son and Spirit, and sets up a gross inequality within the Trinity.

The obvious move would be to say that it is the Trinitarian God, not just the Father, who is ungenerated, self-existent, and the only ultimate cause of everything other than God. This would have the advantage of making a clear distinction between creator and creatures, and eliminate the possibility of having millions of Gods. It would be more clearly monotheistic. But it would undermine the claim that the Father is the generator of God as Trinity.

Other writers (Swinburne is the obvious example) suggest that the persons decide among themselves whose will is to be followed. It is unclear how this would happen, whether it would be decided by majority vote, whether they take turns, or whether all would voluntarily agree to obey the Father, which reverts to the first position. If John of Damascus is followed, however, there would be just one will in God. That suggests that Father, Son, and Spirit make decisions neither on their own nor by joint agreement. Rather, the one creative will of God is a unitary act which is expressed in three differing but complementary forms of instantiation. The will does not exist 'behind' and apart from those forms. It exists and is expressed in them simultaneously. The forms of instantiation each have, in some but not all respects, their own distinctive mode of operation. One way of putting this (not one suggested by, and maybe not acceptable to, Alston) would be to say that the Father is the transcendent originating point of every divine intentional action with regard to the world. The Son or Word is the manifestation or communication of that intention to created beings. The Spirit of God is the universal cooperator with created beings, giving that intention efficacy in the world.

This is one way in which *perichoresis* could be construed – as saying that there are three inseparable and complementary parts of every complex divine action. But it is important that these parts should 'interpenetrate', which usually means that each person knows and feels all that the others know and feel. Of course, God knows the experiences of all finite persons. But in knowing the experiences of other created persons, God is not the fully determining willer or agent of those experiences. No doubt God knows what it is like for other subjects to have experiences, and knows what those experiences are like in the tiniest detail. That knowledge will be part of the divine all-inclusive experience. But such experiences will be known as experiences of other subjects and other wills, which may often differ from God's.

The quality of God's experience and that of the other person will be different. A person's experience will be all the experience that person has. Someone may suffer pain and may feel that pain as intense and affecting all that is known by that person. But when God 'knows' that pain, it will neither be intense for God nor will it affect to any appreciable degree the rest of the divine experience, which will include billions of other experiences too – and much that we cannot begin to comprehend. God may know what it is like for me to feel pain, but that pain cannot affect God in the same way that it affects me. I may be in despair and rage against the pain, but God will not be in despair. The divine beatitude will mitigate the character of my experienced pain and despair by placing it in a much wider context of divine knowledge and goodness. God will be 'distanced' from my pain, affected by it but also affected by huge numbers of other experiences and by God's knowledge of all past and future experiences and possibilities. Such knowledge we cannot begin to imagine.

So God's knowledge of the interior lives of other persons will not simply be a duplicate of those personal experiences as they are experienced by other persons. It will be a 'reflected' knowledge of a unique kind, embracing a total empathy, a 'feeling-with' another, but accompanied by the knowledge that it is the experience of another that is known. In the case of God's knowledge of finite human experiences, part of that otherness will be that human knowledge is sense-based, fallible, limited, and infected by the prejudices and estrangement of human lives from God. Since God suffers no such defects and limitations, it will be quite clear that divine knowledge of human mental contents, however empathetic, will differ in quality from that human knowledge itself.

Most Christians think that God's knowledge of the human experiences of Jesus will not be distanced in the same way as it is from other human experiences, influenced as they are by sin. Since Jesus is sinless and filled with the divine Spirit, God will be able to 'own' Jesus' experiences, to accept them as the experiences of a human fully united to the divine. Thus Jesus' experience on the cross, for instance, will in a special way be both known and acknowledged by God as experiences of the divine in human form. They will express in a definitive way how God shares in the suffering of creatures, and they will define the way in which such suffering can be transformed when human lives become truly united to God.

Given the fact of *perichoresis*, the knowledge each divine person has of the mental contents of the other divine persons will differ from divine knowledge of the content of human minds, even of the human mind of Jesus. For all the Trinitarian persons will be fully omniscient, and nothing will be hidden from any of them. All three have direct access to the minds of the others, so that they all know exactly the same items, even though those items may have originated in different ways and are not known in precisely the same manner.

William Hasker writes that 'the Son has experiences the Father does not have' (Hasker, 2013, p. 193). Only the Son can say, 'I will incarnate' (Hasker, 2013, p. 207), and only the Son experiences suffering and death on the cross. This seems to support the postulate of at least two different sets of experiences and actions, and so two centres of consciousness and will. However, in the case of divine persons, each of these experience-streams will be omnipotent and omniscient. If each divine person is omnipotent, everything that any divine person does must be willed by all divine persons, and if each person is omniscient, everything that any divine person knows must be known by all divine persons.

It follows that it is false that the Son has experiences the Father does not have. It might be better to say that there is just one experience-stream in God, but that stream is complex. Some experiences are the immediate and intuitive and underived experiences of God as creator and sustainer of all. Some experiences are derived from the sense-knowledge of finite beings, including in a special way those derived from Jesus' finite but unique mind. Some experiences are derived from interactive relationships between God and the introspective knowledge of finite beings. These could be called different forms or types of experiences, derived in different ways from different sources – rather as sensory, intellectual, and introspective experiences all go to make up one total human experience, though they can be distinguished as different sorts of experience. You might say that the eyes cause experiences that the ears do not. Yet there are not two 'subjects of experience'. These *two different sorts of experiences*, visual and aural, *originating in different ways*, are obviously integrated into one total human experience.

Using this analogy, we could say that the life of Jesus provides experiences of suffering and learning that are quite different from the creative interactions of the Spirit with many imperfect human minds, and different again from underived and purely divine experiences of knowing all possible worlds and choosing to create one or more of them. Yet these together form one integrated divine experience. When Jesus suffers, the Father empathises and the Spirit strengthens. So we could say that the Father does not suffer as Jesus does on the cross – just as visual experiences are different from aural experiences. Yet the Father suffers by empathy and knows exactly what suffering on the cross is like, because Jesus' experiences are part of the integrated experience of the one divine consciousness.

Similarly, if the Son is not a separate centre of consciousness, the Son will not say, 'I will become incarnate', as though that was an independent decision, taken perhaps after discussion with others. Rather, the one God will say, 'I form the intention that the divine should unite with a human life; I implement this intention by particular acts in relation to Jesus; and I will ensure that this becomes a crucial step towards uniting many human lives to the divine in a particular way.' This is a complex action taken to bring about a desired goal. It can and should be seen as one complex action, and certainly as the action of just one agent acting in different ways to complete the action.

Hasker says that only a person can be a subject of these sorts of experience and action. In that case, it seems very odd to divide the experiences of God between three separate persons. If there were three different persons, would there be anyone who had all those experiences and did all those things? But if the experiences form an overall unity of knowledge, then it seems that they must be experiences of the same person – or, in the case of God, the same supra-personal being with many personal properties.

As well as completely sharing every experience, the divine persons will necessarily be coexistent and cooperative, in different and complementary ways, in every divine act. If the Father did not send Jesus (make known to Jesus the divine will) and the Spirit did not support him, then Jesus would not have manifested the will of

God on the cross. All three agree in willing that event, and all three are fully aware of what it is like to undergo it. But they co-act and co-experience in different specific ways – the Father grieving, the Son suffering, and the Spirit strengthening.

We no longer have three identical individuals of one kind, inseparably united and interpenetrating in a mysterious way. We have one will and experience of God, necessarily instantiated in different forms by Father, Son, and Spirit. We can say, with Alston, that God is three persons in one substance. But this will no longer be best expressed by saying that there are three identical individuals (first substance) sharing one divine nature (second substance). Once we have added Alston's additional provisos – which, as Sarah Coakley shows in her discussion of Gregory of Nyssa (Coakley, 1999), can be found in the writings of the Cappadocians in their very different historical contexts – we can say that God is one substance, one individual and personal subject of action and experience. There are three ways in which this substance is manifested – call them 'persons' in a special, technical, and unique sense – each of which manifests 'one operation and will' in its own distinctive way. It is true that the Son becomes incarnate and suffers, whereas the Father does not. But in those acts the Father is acting as sustainer and the Spirit is acting as inner strengthener. The Son is implementing the will of the Father, not a different and discrete will of his own. The Father does not experience the suffering of the Son as the suffering of an 'other', from which the Father distances himself. If *perichoresis* exists, the Father and Spirit will experience the suffering of the Son.

Consider how in Jesus a human person can be one with the divine, yet human and divine natures seem to be wholly different. You can say that the human Jesus grows and eats and learns, while God the Word does not grow, eat, or die. Yet in Jesus humanity and the Word are united. The traditional approach was to say that we have to speak of one being with two natures, or what I have called 'aspects' of the same compound reality, which are united as closely as possible, though exactly what that unity consists in remains deeply mysterious and unique. You can use the same sort of approach to say that the eternal Father and the eternal Word are different aspects of the same compound reality, united in the closest possible way and yet not confused. We might then say that God does not suffer as the Father. But God suffers as the incarnate Word, and God as Father knows what this suffering is like. Both the Father and the Word will thus suffer, though the Word suffers in human flesh, while the Father suffers by fully empathetic knowledge. In a similar way, the Spirit cooperates synergistically with human wills in a way that the Father does not. But God as Father knows and feels what it is like for God as Spirit to do so and shares in willing the actions of the Spirit.

God as Father remains transcendent to all creation. God as Son manifests in creation. God as Spirit unites creation to the divine. It is one God, one omniscient and omnipotent being, who has these three aspects or modes of being. It is the threefold God who is omnipotent in the uniquely strong sense that God is the source of everything other than God and can intend and create without reference to any other being. The Father, the Word, and the Spirit have no independent wills, since they necessarily will all things in common. They have no private knowledge, since each person knows all that the others think and do. But they have different sources of knowledge (as transcendent, incarnate, and immanent in created things), and they do different things (support all things, suffer, and strive within human hearts). Word and Spirit implement the Father's will in particular ways, unique to them. Moreover, they necessarily cooperate in every divine action, contributing a particular element to every divine action (sustaining, manifesting, and cooperatively inspiring), which in every case is the action of all of them together. A 'divine person' in this sense is not an individual substance of a rational nature – or at least that is an inadequate and misleading way of putting it. A divine person is a necessarily inseparable, complementary, and interconnected co-agent in every divine action, having no independent knowledge or will but implementing the will of God in a distinctive form of action and experience proper to it. Each person is a co-consciousness and co-agency, and inseparably together they constitute the one ungenerated and unrestrictedly omnipotent source of all.

The analogy of self-giving love between three individuals is not a good analogy either on a three-consciousness or on a one-consciousness account, for such love only exists between God and beings other than God. We speak of Trinity because it articulates how it is that the finite creation is united to participate in the divine. The decisive reason for there being three persons in God is because *theosis* is the purpose of creation, and the heart of Christian faith. This universe is created in order that autonomous persons can come into existence, can shape their own lives freely and creatively, and can find their fulfilment in being united to the divine in love. The eternal Trinity in relation to the created world manifests itself as the transcendent creator, the archetype and ideal of creation (believed to be manifest on this planet and in human form in Jesus), and the creative power that unites creation to its divine source. It is primarily because of this revelatory self-disclosure that we think of God as Trinity.

CHAPTER 37

The Convergence of Social and One-Consciousness Models of the Trinity

The English philosophical theologian David Brown also prefers the conceptual model of three individuals of the same divine nature who are necessarily bound together in unity of action, or what he calls 'unity of operations' (Brown, 1985, p. 279). These individuals are 'three distinct centres of consciousness, each with its own distinctive mental content' (Brown, 1985, p. 289). By this he means that the Spirit derives knowledge of human hearts 'from the inside', as it inspires and transforms human lives; the Son experiences physical pain and human emotions, and the Father knows the cosmos as a whole. The Spirit and the Father do not suffer physically on the cross, and the Son, now enthroned in glory, does not act dynamically within nature and human lives to unite those lives to the divine.

At the same time, he writes, 'though they have separate powers, to know the mind and will of one is to know that of all three' (Brown, 1985, p. 293). This entails *perichoresis* in the fullest sense. It means that there is no experience of a divine person that is not known by all three, and there is no action or intention of a divine person that is not shared by all three. For instance, when the Spirit cooperates with a human will, and when it derives distinctive experiences from such cooperation, this is a distinctive mental content in that the Father and the Son do not directly initiate those actions or receive in an unmediated way those experiences.

Yet they concur in initiating those actions, and both know exactly what it is like to have those experiences, wholly empathise with them, and accept them as their own. Moreover, each action and experience is only what it is precisely because these three subject/agents act together in cooperative, essential, and complementary ways in every action and experience. When the Spirit inspires some human mind, the Father wills that this should occur and sustains that human mind in being, and the Son provides the pattern of life which the Spirit takes as its goal.

Brown briefly but significantly suggests that when the three persons act together in such ways (as they necessarily do), 'the attributes that are unique to divinity are distributed among three persons rather than one' (Brown, 1985, p. 300). He means that those attributes are 'most appropriately applied to the Godhead as a whole' and that such attribution to the totality is different from, and richer than, attribution to the persons separately. He points out that only the Trinity as a whole is truly omnipotent, in the sense of being unlimited by anything other than itself (since each person is limited by having to agree with the others). Only the Trinity as a whole is truly omniscient (since each person lacks the knowledge which the other persons have that some knowledge is their own, even though each person knows everything the others know in some sense). And only the Trinity as a whole can be good in the 'full richness of meaning' which comes from seeing all the 'distinctive aspects of the activity of the three persons' together – that is, from seeing their mutually supportive acts taken as a whole.

Although Brown says that he prefers a 'plurality model' of the Trinity to a 'unity model', it turns out that the plurality model as he construes it (three subjects in complete unity of mind and will, having mutually complementary and inseparable actions and experiences) is virtually equivalent to the unity model (one subject in three different but complementary and inseparable modes of subsistence). As was usually held in the Patristic period, the Trinity only acts towards things outside it as a whole – *Opera trinitatis ad extra sunt indivisi* – though different 'persons' take what we might call leading roles in all such actions. Each person acts in a distinctive way, though all persons act 'as one', and each person knows everything the other persons know, though they do not each gain that knowledge in the same way. So the persons do not have different mental content in the sense that they might each know quite different things, and they do not initiate different actions in the sense that they might do quite different things. They know the same things, do the same things, and always and necessarily act together as one. It seems to me that to say this is one God in different forms is rather less misleading than to say that it is three individuals (who might be called 'gods') bound together as a small society. It is less misleading because it clearly preserves a commitment to monotheism and because it dispenses with the questions of why the divine society should be so very small, of how one can be sure that its members will never disagree, and of how one can be sure that they will all cooperate in every action in precisely the ways that are essential to the full nature of that action even though they are supposed to be distinct centres of consciousness.

Brown comes very near to saying this when he writes that we might best describe the Trinity by 'ascribing consciousness to the persons and self-consciousness to the Godhead' (Brown, 1989, p. 73). I have to admit that I find that suggestion rather unclear, especially since 'self-consciousness' is not closely defined. The persons will surely be self-conscious in being aware of their own existence. And Brown seems to associate 'self-consciousness' with reflection and a sort of disengaged search for justification of one's decisions. I cannot think of God the Trinity as needing to be disengaged or reflective in this sense. So I find the distinction Brown is seeking as more helpfully put when he says that the persons share a 'social vision and purpose' and are 'modifications of the social whole' (Brown, 1989, p. 72). That whole 'has no existence in itself' – it is not a sort of 'fourth more inclusive person' who is needed to unite the separate experiences of the other three. The 'social whole' exists 'only as mediated through and expressed in' the three persons.

I am reminded here of the early twentieth-century Oxford school of Absolute Idealism. This school saw the whole of human history, and the individual members of it, as appearances of the progressive self-development of the Absolute, which was precisely mediated through and expressed in individual persons but somehow was the true reality of which individuals were the appearances. It is noteworthy, however, that 'the Absolute' of philosophers such as F. H. Bradley was impersonal and lacked most of the characteristics of a personal and loving God. For Christians, God needs to be distinguished more clearly from human individuals than this. Human persons are not just parts of the Absolute. God is a distinct and fully personal reality which is capable of fully relational love from which created persons can be alienated or to which they can be united while retaining their independent human form of being.

I am also wary of speaking of a 'social whole' as a fully real existent which is greater and more valuable than the sum of its parts. I think we need a more unitary and fully personal model of God, as a being to whom humans can relate in love without being merely parts of God. Human persons are essentially other than God, not parts of God. God is not a social whole, and if God has a vision and purpose, that vision and purpose is conceived and executed by one fully personal subject of action and experience.

It is not the product of a society of persons. A society is a product of a developing history of individual personal interactions, and therefore I do not think the uncreated and unoriginated God can be thought of as a society.

However, I do agree with Brown that God's vision and purpose is mediated through and expressed in a distinctively threefold form as it gives rise to a created universe. When Brown says that the divine self 'resides in the Godhead as a whole' (Brown, 1989, p. 51), we have left behind a social view of the Trinity. The self or personal being of God does reside in the Trinity as a whole, and the divine persons are three distinct but inseparable, coordinate, and complementary ways of acting and knowing, of mediating the actions of God in and receiving the knowledge of God from the created world.

A number of recent writers who think of themselves as supporters of a 'social' Trinity exhibit a similar ambiguity between social and one-consciousness views. The Roman Catholic cardinal and theologian Walter Kasper writes, 'It is clear that the unity of being in God entails unity of consciousness' (Kasper, 1984, p. 288). So there is one consciousness in God, which entails one centre of will and subject of experience. This one consciousness exists 'in a triple mode': 'there are three personal i.e. distinct manners in which the divine substance subsists' (Kasper, 1984, p. 296). The terminology of 'modes' and 'manners' is reminiscent of Rahner and Barth, and does not suggest three distinct subjects of consciousness.

Yet Kasper says that there are 'three subjects who are reciprocally conscious of each other'. Indeed, he defends the traditional term 'person' for these three subjects, because he is convinced of the importance of the view that persons necessarily exist in relation. Kasper writes: 'an isolated unipersonal God is inconceivable', for a personal God must exist in relation to another. So he develops the idea that the persons of the Trinity are in a fully interpersonal loving relationship to one another – God is love, and 'love cannot be otherwise conceived' (Kasper, 1984, p. 309). In this relationship, 'the father is purely a giver and a sender . . . the Son is . . . the mediator . . . a pure passing-on . . . the Spirit is pure receiving' (Kasper, 1984, p. 309). Such love is the pure and total giving of being 'that surrenders and bestows itself'. Because God is personal, and because persons can only exist in relation, Kasper writes that 'the Trinity is the only possible and consistent form of monotheism' (Kasper, 1984, p. 295), a form which sees the unity of the divine being in terms of a loving communion of persons.

It is hard not to be moved by this vision of a being of total love which is the fullness of love in its own eternal being. In a sovereign and free act of self-giving, it brings into existence a universe of creatures who are deeply loved and destined to share in that love which is the life of the Trinity. Unfortunately, the logical problems of the view are forbidding. If there is a unity of will and experience in God, there cannot be three separate centres of will and experience, though it is not too difficult to think of three different modes of willing and experiencing. As Gregory of Nyssa suggested, the Father could intend an action, the Son could effect it, and the Spirit could complete it. These three forms of intention and experience would together form the 'mental content' of one subject of action and experience. That seems more intelligible than trying to think of three subjects wholly sharing all intentions and experiences, and yet being different subjects of consciousness.

Most revealingly, the 'persons' of the Trinity never act alone, and so they cannot individually be properly referred to as 'God' (the New Testament does refer to the Father as God, but it is always the case that this is short for 'God the Father' and in no way implies that only the Father is God or that the Father could exist alone). The one agent of all divine acts is the Trinity, and recognition of this fact resolves some problems that arise if all divine persons are said to be agents, each of whom is identical with God.

CHAPTER 38

Life-Streams and Persons

These problems are stated strongly by the philosopher David Wiggins (Wiggins, 1980), who argued that the doctrine of the Trinity was incoherent because it held that the Father is the same God as the Son but not the same person as the Son. Indeed, the Athanasian Creed states that 'the Father is God, the Son is God, and the Holy Ghost is God, and yet they are not three Gods, but one God'. But, Wiggins argued, if two things are identical, then they must be identical with one another in every respect. However, this charge can be evaded if one says that no person, or aspect, of the Trinity is strictly identical with God. Each person is identical with an aspect of God, and so in a sense one could say, with the Athanasian Creed that 'each person is God'. But the 'is' here is not the 'is' of strict identity. It is an 'is' of inclusion, like saying that 'each person is divine, or has the nature of God'. The Father is not, however, strictly identical with God in Wiggin's sense of possessing every property that God has. Nor is the Son, and nor is the Spirit. So the Father is not 'the same God as the Son'. The Father and the Son are not gods at all. They have the nature of God. But the one God is an inseparable composite of Father, Son, and Spirit, as we clearly discern when we see that the Trinity always acts as a whole in relation to created things. It is never the case that the Father, Son, or Spirit acts on its own. That is why we can correctly say that God dies on the cross, not just that Jesus dies on the cross. Yet it is true that it is Jesus who goes to the cross and who suffers the pains of his body. In other words, it is Jesus as God united to a human person who suffers on the cross and who contributes suffering to the experience of God. This is also why, if we are concerned for technical correctness, it may be better not to say that Jesus is identical with God just like that. Jesus is identical with the Word; even that is a special sense of 'identity' – we have to say that there is something which has the properties of both the eternal Word and of the human Jesus. But the Word is not strictly identical with God. The Word is one essential aspect or mode of God as God relates to humans. This implies, however, that the Word, the Spirit, and the Father are not distinct persons or subjects, but rather distinct manners in which the one subject, the Trinitarian God, exists.

It is perhaps by now clear that the word 'person' as used by social Trinitarians is not, despite what they tend to say, very much at all like the word 'person' as used with regard to human subjects of consciousness. Sometimes it is hard to tell the difference between 'person' and 'mode of being', which is supposed to mark an important distinction between social and one-substance views of the Trinity.

For instance, when Brian Leftow writes that God is one person which contains three 'life-streams', or streams of experience and action (Leftow, 2009); when William Craig writes that God is one substance with 'three complete sets of rational cognitive faculties'(Craig, 2009); and when William Hasker says that 'one concrete divine nature' supports three 'life-streams', it is hard to tell them apart. This is the case even though Leftow writes as a 'substance' theorist and Hasker and Craig regard themselves as 'social' theorists. In fact, in this example I think that Leftow turns out to be more like a social theorist, even as he claims to be defending a substance view. He expressly states that the three life-streams have no internal access to one another ('God as father has no internal access to and is not thinking the thoughts of God as Son': Leftow, 2004, p. 312), and that means that the three do think and act independently, which is all you want (and probably more than you want) for a social view. For a thoroughgoing substance theorist, all persons would have total access to one another and would engage in the same thoughts as one another – because they would be the thoughts of the very same personal subject. Craig and Hasker, on the other hand, seem like substance Trinitarians, since there is only one divine soul-substance (for Craig) or numerically identical 'trope', or uniquely instantiated divine nature (for Hasker), respectively. Yet what else can a soul, or what else can a uniquely instantiated personal nature, be than a person?

William Hasker introduces what he calls the Trinitarian Possibility Postulate (Hasker, 2013, p. 228), that 'a single concrete divine nature can support three distinct lives'. A 'concrete nature' is not just a property, but rather what Hasker calls a 'trope', a unique bearer of the properties which constitute a divine nature. So the divine substance (bearer of the divine properties) can support three continuing streams of consciousness and agency.

One chief analogy he uses to support this idea is that of multiple personalities in one human being (Hasker, 2013, p. 235). Significantly, however, he says that these are not many different persons, but instead 'multiple centres of consciousness' of one person, and therapy has the aim of uniting them in one integrated personality. The suggestion is, then, that one personal substance may support three 'streams of consciousness', some of which may be aware of the others' thoughts and acts. This is not a perfection of personality, however. The personalities do not usually love each other, and it is generally thought better to have one integrated personality.

So I am inclined to accept the Trinitarian Possibility Postulate but suggest that it would not be a good situation for God to be in.

If the three 'streams' are wholly aware of each other and wholly concur in each other's actions (as *perichoresis* entails), it is simpler to say that there is one stream of consciousness operating in three significantly different ways of relating to creation. There is one wholly integrated divine consciousness and will with three necessary, inseparable, and complementary modes of activity. Hasker himself says, 'Each person is wholly God, but each person is not the whole of God' (Hasker, 2013, p. 251). As I would put it, each divine person is part of the one consciousness and will of God.

I have said that I think it is too anthropomorphic to say that God is really 'a person', though God includes personal properties such as knowing and willing. Thus God can be regarded analogically as a personal subject, and so the three basic different types of relational activity in which God engages are not the actions of separate agents.

Does it follow that there is then no mutual love between Father and Son? It does. There cannot be mutual love between two aspects of divine experience and action. Love only truly exists where there is an 'other' to receive and return love. Of course, the human Jesus is just such an other, so there is mutual love between Father and the human aspect of the incarnate Son. This emphasises the point that the eternal Word is not a separate Subject from the Father. But Jesus is precisely a separate Subject, though one who has been subsumed from the first moment of his human life into the divine life. Thus there is mutual love between the infinite God and the human who is assumed into the divine life but not obliterated by that life.

It is in this way that the Incarnation of God expresses a quite distinctive perspective on the relation of God and created reality. The Incarnation is sometimes seen as the descent of a limitlessly powerful God into the world of humanity, and of course in a sense this is what it is. But it is also, and equally importantly, the assumption of human life into the divine life. The classical tradition is quite clear about this, because it insists that at the Incarnation nothing changed in God (since the divine nature is immutable), and all changes occurred in the human nature of Jesus. It was not so much that God 'became' man as that this man was transformed to be one with the divine. If we accept a temporalist idea of God, the same point can be made, with the addition of the claim that God does change by taking this human nature into the divine life. This accords with the axiom that if anything is added to the divine, that entails some sort of change in the divine, since the divine has some additional properties that it did not always have and does not necessarily have.

Moreover, this also implies that humans – or at least one human – become part of the divine life. Human nature and divine nature cannot be seen as totally separate from one another, for in Jesus they are united indissolubly.

In early Patristic theology, expressed most clearly in Eastern Orthodox traditions, this was not just a matter of one unique human individual being united to the divine. For, in Platonic fashion, human nature was seen as ontologically real, as something in which all humans participate. Thus when human nature was united in Jesus to the divine nature, it was humanity as such, and in essence, that was united to the divine. In other words, any who share in this human nature are thereby united to the divine. The Platonic view is complicated by the fact that this new human nature has to be imparted to those who already participate in the 'fallen' Adamic human nature, and it has usually been assumed that not all will accept that impartation – not all will be 'saved'.

A transfer has to be made between the estranged nature of humanity and the new unity of divine and human which was made real in Jesus. There are deep theological disputes about just how this transfer is to be made, and about whether it applies to all or some humans, but what is generally agreed among Christians is that it can only be made by God and that its possibility is assured by the death and resurrection of Jesus. Humans exist either without Christ, and thus without the true light and life of humankind, or they exist 'in Christ' and are then reborn into a renewed human nature.

The Christian hope is that all humans (or all humans who respond positively) will eventually participate in the union between humans and the divine which was accomplished in Christ. The first Letter to Timothy says that 'God our Saviour . . . desires everyone to be saved and to come to the knowledge of the truth' (1 Timothy 2, 4). What God desires must be a real possibility, even if its fulfilment cannot be guaranteed. That is a good reason for thinking that all humans may become 'participants in the divine nature' (2 Peter 1, 4). That participation, however, is not adequately conceived as a matter of gaining admission to a divine society of three. Hasker says, 'the disciples of Jesus are actually drawn into the personal relationships within the Trinity' (Hasker, 2013, p. 212). But there are no such relationships. *Theosis*, or sharing the nature of God, is not like joining an elite social club as another member. It is being fully indwelt by the Spirit, being united in a communion of being with Christ, and knowing and loving the ultimate ground of all being as 'Father'. However this is construed, the relation to each divine 'person' is different, and in no case is it a relation of one person to another person of the same sort. It is a combination of being indwelt by the divine, of indwelling the divine reality, and of relationship to a vastly supra-human creator. It is a threefold way of being related to one undivided but internally complex divine reality.

Belief in the Trinity is not just a very abstruse theoretical matter of deciding on the exact inner nature of a postulated supreme being.

It is a way of living in relation to a reality which fulfils and perfects human life. It is this practical threefold dynamic relationship to God which is central, in practice, to the doctrine of the Trinity. In it, humans encounter God as the one and only origin of all things, as primordial and transcendent initiator. They encounter God as the implementer of the divine plan and the self-expressive unfolding of the divine will manifest in Jesus as the human form of the divine, the embodied Ideal of human personhood. And they encounter God as the completer and goal of creation, as immanent integrator and cooperative unifier of created reality with the divine. Each set of mental cognitive/affective powers requires the existence of the two other modes of being for its existence and activity, and the bearer or subject of these three sets is the indivisible substance of the one and only divine being.

CHAPTER 39

Modalism and Necessity

Every attempt to give a coherent account of the Trinity has to balance on a knife edge between saying that there are three gods and saying that there is only one God who just appears in different modes to different people at different times. It is obvious that if the account I have given tilts too far in one direction, it is in the direction of the latter affirmation, of what is often called modalism. I therefore need to give some exposition of what is inadequate about modalism and of how my account avoids it.

Most orthodox Christians do not doubt that there is only one God, and they speak of the Trinity as three persons in one substance. So what is needed to represent a reasonably orthodox view is for us to say *how* God can be one substance and three persons. William Hasker proposes that we can speak about God as three individuals of one uniquely instantiated divine nature. On his view, we can speak of mutual loving relations between these individuals, but we probably need a rather radical revision of the Patristic claim that the divine being is simple and immutable. However, I feel that such a revision is needed if we are to think of Father, Son, and Spirit as persons in anything like the sense of distinct centres of consciousness and will. I also feel that this is not in any way a rejection of the Patristic concern to be true to Biblical statements of the relation between Jesus, the one he addressed as 'Father', and the Spirit who was 'sent' by Father and Son. It is a matter of using different philosophical concepts in order to describe these relations more adequately.

However, I object to describing the three divine persons as distinct centres of consciousness and will, and have instead described them as 'aspects' or 'forms of being' of one divine consciousness and will, one personal being. But is this just modalism, which is usually explained as precisely saying that the divine persons are aspects or modes of one God?

As I have continually complained, it is very difficult to find suitable words to use when you are trying to describe relationships which are unique and probably beyond complete human understanding. What you have to do is try to draw distinctions between different meanings that words may have and point out what may be helpful and what may be misleading in choosing the words you do.

What, then, is objectionable about modalism? As it is usually explained, modalism affirms that there is one personal God (nothing wrong so far!) who can appear in a number of different ways to different people and at different times. Some Hindus believe that there is one supreme Lord who can appear as different Gods – Vishnu, Shiva, and Kali, for example. It does not matter much which God people choose to worship, since they are all appearances of the same Lord in the end. Personal choice will reflect different temperaments, different concerns, and different experiences. That could properly be called a modalist view, and it would not be acceptable to most Christians. These appearances are optional for God, presumably, and temporary, and they are visions which are attuned to the minds of the devotees, not essential and permanent properties of God.

Christian modalists may assert that there is just one God who appears either as Father, or as Son, or as Spirit but is not actually any of these things. The appearances are often thought to be successive. So the Father becomes the Son in the Incarnation and becomes the Spirit after the Resurrection. The three 'persons' are like masks which God may put on or take off for specific purposes – a position which the words *persona* or *prosopon* readily suggest. This position would be denied if it was held that God really is threefold essentially and originally, permanently, indissolubly, and irreducibly. It is not an *option* for God to be threefold – that is what God essentially is. And God is not sometimes one person and sometimes another – God is always threefold.

The position I hold is not modalist, in this meaning of the word, because God is essentially threefold. I have said, however, that God might not be known as 'Father, Son, and Spirit' in worlds where there were no fathers, sons, atmospheres, flames, or birds. These are all symbols for God drawn from things common on this planet. Other worlds may find other symbols, which we cannot be expected to imagine, that are more appropriate for them. The question is whether these symbols are appropriate symbols for some real underlying threefoldness in God.

I think it is clear that the word 'Father' does not apply literally to God, since a father is a genetically male parent with a Y chromosome, and God the Father does not have a gender, or even a body. For this reason, the symbol 'Father' is found misleading even by some human beings, for it suggests to many people that males are somehow more like God than females – a suggestion I would find offensive. Accordingly, if you ask if God is essentially a Father, I would have to say no. For it all depends on what the symbol of fatherhood suggests to particular persons, and to some people it would unfortunately suggest cruelty or ruthless authority, which I think would be quite misleading.

However, the word 'Father', especially in combination with the other terms used of God by Christian believers, can suggest – and

I think that it properly does suggest – creation and care. Good fathers on earth are a source of the being of their children, and they care for them and for their good. In speaking of God as father, then, we are pointing to an aspect of the divine being which is the source of the whole physical universe and which cares for the good of what it has generated.

Similarly, in speaking of God as 'Son' we are pointing to a different aspect of the divine being which enters into a specific relation of love with one (or more) created persons. This is God embodied in creation and expressing the divine nature in finite form. That form does not have to be human. It could be any form of being which is capable of expressing more-or-less well the divine nature.

In the case of Jesus, the Son is not only the embodiment of God, 'God with us' (Matthew 1, 23), but also the redeemer, the one who liberates humans from sin. By his self-sacrificial love, culminating in the giving of his life on the cross, and by his victory over death, manifested in his resurrection, he delivers human nature from slavery to sin and unites it to the divine life. This deliverance is made available to human beings throughout the ages by the 'Spirit', which transforms human lives from within until they too achieve full union with the divine. The egoism and hatred which is such a marked feature of human lives are burned away, and God's love comes to fill the human form. This is a third real and essential aspect of God: acting inwardly in human lives to unite them to God.

The terms used for these three aspects – Father, Son, and Spirit – are terms drawn wholly from, and dependent for their meaning upon, items in a specifically human world. God takes human form, God suffers and dies because of the actions of human agents, and God liberates from the endemic evil that marks human nature. Yet God did not have to create humans, humans did not have to become prey to hatred and greed, and God did not have to deliver humans by death on a cross. These things happened, and they mark ways in which God creates, humans fall into evil, and God redeems them. But these are all contingent occurrences. They did not have to happen. God might well have created other kinds of intelligent life, there could have been intelligent life that did not fall into evil, and God might have chosen another way of reuniting the human species to the divine.

I am inclined to say that God did create other kinds of intelligent life and that it would be very odd if in all the galaxies in this universe there are no other kinds of intelligent life. The point I am making about the contingency of God's specific creation and relation to created beings on this planet does not depend upon there actually being such other forms of life. It may be true that humans are the only intelligent beings in the whole universe. The evolutionary palaeontologist Simon Conway-Morris argues that in our universe, given the basic laws and constants upon which it has developed, carbon-based humanoids are the only sorts of intelligent beings that can exist. He further argues that the conditions for the existence of such life are so extremely rare that we are probably the only intelligent beings that exist even in a universe as large and old as this one (Conway Morris, 2003, subtitled 'Inevitable Humans in a Lonely Universe').

It is extremely difficult, if not impossible, to calculate probabilities in this area. I can only say that I will be quite disappointed if Conway-Morris is right. My understanding of the unlimited love and power of God is such that I would think it quite possible for God to create many kinds of intelligent beings, and quite probable that God has done so. But of course I have to admit that I really do not know, and I do not suppose that God has any obligation to do everything that God could possibly do.

What I am confident about, however, is that, logically speaking, there seems to be nothing incoherent in supposing that many sorts of intelligent beings could exist (Christians have, after all, often believed that there are angels and other 'heavenly powers'). And if God's creation of this universe is free, then God might have created other universes. That makes the creation of this universe contingent, something God did not have to do. From this alone, it follows that the terms we use to describe the Trinity, insofar as they depend upon contingent matters of fact, cannot denote necessary and essential properties of God. It may seem a radical and to some an incredible and unnecessary claim that extraterrestrial intelligences exist. But it is not at all incredible, and it has in fact been part of most traditional Christian beliefs to say that God did not have to create this universe, that humans did not have to sin, and that God could have redeemed humans without becoming incarnate. Thomas Aquinas certainly asserted all these propositions. So my argument does not depend upon positing extra-terrestrial beings, though our very recent discovery of the vast extent of the universe does help the imagination think that God may really be known by other beings in very different ways than those in which God is known by us.

This may seem to be moving back to a form of modalism, since it now seems that God appears as Father, Son, and Spirit to humans but might not do so to other beings. Or to put it another way, the immanent God, God in the divine being itself, may not be adequately describable as Father, Son, and Spirit. That does sound as if these are just appearances to us and not essential characteristics of God, whether or not God is related to us.

That is why, in Part III of this book, I wanted to distinguish clearly between the economic and the immanent Trinity. But I did still talk about an immanent 'Trinity', not about a Unitarian God.

What is contingent is God appearing to us as Father, Son, and Spirit. But Barth and Rahner are right in thinking that if this is how God truly is in relation to us, then that must express something true about the divine being in itself. Immanuel Kant is probably the best-known philosopher who made a distinction between 'things-in-themselves' and 'things as they appear to us'. His stated view is that we can know nothing, theoretically, about things in themselves and that all human knowledge is confined to appearances. He was, however, unable to maintain this view consistently, since he did think of the 'noumenal' world of things in themselves as real, existent, and the cause of appearances – and these are all categories which are supposed to apply only to appearances. He also thought of the noumenal world as rational, intelligible, and good, though he tried to explain that these were postulates of reason rather than items that could be theoretically known.

It is very difficult to speak about something of which you claim to know absolutely nothing. Indeed, I think it is self-contradictory. The question is this: what does our knowledge of God in relation to humans entitle us to say about God in the divine being itself? I think one certainly has to say that God is the cause of all genuine appearances of the divine in the world. But acceptance of the authenticity of an economic Trinity compels one to say more. God is capable of taking form within the created world and of enabling that world to participate in the divine life. There is not a complete separation or ontological chasm between God and the world. God is such that the created world and the divine can be united. That is, God is able to create and to appear in finite forms and to embrace these appearances in the primal origin. This is a form of threefoldness in God – primordial being and origin, expression or appearance, and participation or inclusion of appearances in the primordial origin.

It is not therefore a denial of Christian Trinitarianism to speak of God as creator, redeemer, and sanctifier. It is a reminder that the specific ways in which God comes to humans is only one way in which God is in relation to creation. Nevertheless, underlying that way is an essential threefoldness in God, which is neither accidental nor temporary nor merely apparent. It may sound modalist to say that the persons in God are modes or forms of being of one God. But it is not. The specific modalities of Father, Son, and Spirit are appearances to us in our world. But they manifest an essential threefoldness of the divine, an 'immanent Trinity' which belongs to Being itself.

If that is so, does it mean that there must always be some creation, that God cannot exist without creation? I do not think that is an entailment of what I have said. The specific form of *agape* love which Jesus discloses is a specific fulfilment of the divine nature. But on a temporalist view of God, there can be and there is change in God, and the sort of self-giving and sacrificial love which Jesus manifests can only exist in worlds of creation where personal beings are estranged from God. Though some theologians postulate that such estrangement is a necessary part of the process of the creation of those who are genuinely other than God, a strong view of moral freedom would suggest that sin is not necessary to finite personal beings as such. If Jesus is sinless, there is certainly a relationship of love between the Father and the person of Jesus, and this suggests that divine love does not have to be expressed in suffering and sacrifice. God can be essentially loving without having to manifest every possible way in which love could be expressed. All that needs to be true is that God manifests love in the way appropriate to the sorts of situations that exist – and God will decide what exists.

So it could be that God could be more like an Aristotelian self-sufficient God while being essentially loving. God could be the subject within whom all possibilities exist, the creative actualisation of many forms of goodness within the divine being itself, and the love of actualised goodness, the appreciation and integration of goodness into the divine experience. The difference from an Aristotelian conception is that such a being of supreme self-contemplating value could express itself by generating others who could share in the contemplation of good and who could also contribute new forms of value which could not exist in the divine being alone – values of genuine relationship, cooperation, and mutual creativity.

Is it necessary that God should create in this way? In a masterly analysis of Aquinas' *Summa Contra Gentiles*, Norman Kretzmann has argued that it is. He cites the 'Dionysian principle' (which he shows that Aquinas accepts in more than one place), which is that 'Goodness is by its very nature diffusive of itself and (thereby) of being'. If the will of God is 'the absolutely universal appetite for what is good' (Kretzmann, 1997, p. 197), then this will is 'by nature' diffusive of many forms of goodness.

Kretzmann points out that Aquinas writes, 'In willing himself, God wills all the things that are in him ... in willing himself, therefore, God also wills other things' (Aquinas, *Summa Contra Gentiles*, 75.643, cited in Kretzmann, p. 218).

For Aquinas, God is non-temporal, so whatever God wills, God wills always. Further, God's being is both necessary and simple, so God could not will otherwise than God does, and it is not possible for God to will some things contingently and other things necessarily. Of course, Aquinas also insists that God's creation of this universe is freely chosen, but Kretzmann holds that this is an inconsistency. Since God's will is identical with God's essence, then if God wills to create, God essentially (necessarily) wills to create.

We could hold that God's creation is free in that there are innumerable other worlds that God could have created – it is not self-contradictory to say that they could exist. But God's willing of God's own being, which is admitted to be necessary, includes the fact that God also wills all that God does. In the *Summa Theologiae*, Aquinas writes, 'Every agent, to the extent to which it is in actuality and perfect, produces something like itself' (Aquinas, *Summa Theologiae*, 1a, 19, 2c). Not only so, but God wills a specific created world, and this will could not be otherwise.

This is a problem for Aquinas, and Kretzmann proposes a resolution of it by saying, 'God's will is necessitated as regards *whether* to create, but fully free as regards *what* to create' (Kretzmann, p. 224).

That proposal requires that we admit complexity and temporality into the divine being and say that the divine will is necessary in some respects but contingent in others. I do of course accept that. My only reservation is that I do not think God can be obliged to generate every possible sort of good. So how much good must be diffused, according to the Dionysian principle? Perhaps one should be a little more cautious and say only that it would be good for God to create other agents, but it is not absolutely essential for God to do so since God could envisage, create, and love many forms of goodness without creating any finite persons. This would mean that we would not be committed to saying that there could not be a God without creation. Divine threefoldness, a trinity of envisagement, actualisation, and love is essential to the divine being. It naturally, but not quite necessarily, expands into a Trinity of other-creation, relationship, and inclusion. And in our world it further expands into a Trinity rightly described as comprising a compassionate Father, a redemptive and self-sacrificial Son, and a sanctifying Spirit.

Such a view entails that God acts in genuinely creative and responsive ways in, and is affected by, events in the created world.

It stands in opposition to much traditional thinking about the changeless perfection of God. In that respect it agrees with the usual thesis of social Trinitarians that God is in some distinctive sense changing and thus temporal. It also agrees with the 'social' view that God relates to us in *agapistic* love and that such love can only be realised in relation to others.

This economic Trinity, the Trinity of Father, Son, and Spirit that we humans experience, is rooted in a threefoldness of subjectivity, creativity, and unitive love which is not strictly identical with the Trinity as it is expressed in the human world. That in turn is rooted in a deeper 'immanent' threefoldness of primal origin, expressed thought, and beatific love. It is not a society of three distinct individuals. If this view is maintained, unnecessary problems can be avoided about how 'otherness' can exist within the being of God, about whether God can really be a society, about why that society is so small, and about how a society of more-or-less identical omnipotent and omniscient beings can love each other in any meaningful sense. Most importantly, we can unhesitatingly affirm the words of Jesus: 'Hear, O Israel, the Lord your God is one Lord'.

CHAPTER 40

The Cosmic Trinity

There have been three main themes running throughout this discussion of God as Trinity. One is that the idea of the Trinity as a society of three subjects of consciousness, although it can seem emotionally appealing, is logically and theologically inadequate and that in any case in its most rigorously worked-out versions it converges with the more traditional one-consciousness view. A second is that the God who was incarnate in Jesus is revealed as a dynamic, creative, responsive, and relational God whose revealed nature as 'love' points to a divine movement to create and love other persons. The 'social Trinity' hypothesis is right about this, though it is not really satisfactory to try to place that 'other' within the being of God. The third theme is that God, as creator of the cosmos, cannot be fully and finally understood in the rather anthropocentric images familiar to human beings on this planet. What God has revealed to us of the divine being, while it is absolutely true in relation to us and our understanding, is far from enabling us to comprehend the glory and majesty of the divine being in itself. God, we may say with the Anglican theologian John Macquarrie, is the name of that Mystery which sets a goal of supreme value to the cosmos, mediates signs of that goal and value to those who are open to perceive them, and evokes a commitment to hope that the goal can ultimately be realised.

I think it is clear that Macquarrie's suggestions are derived from his belief that an authentic sign of the moral goal of human existence was present and manifest in Jesus and that Jesus' suffering love and resurrection prefigures, for Christians, that goal and the way to it. This can be put by saying that God can be correctly described as existing in threefold form.

God, writes Macquarrie, is the primordial source of all possibilities of being. God is 'poured out through expressive Being, giving rise to the world of particular beings'. And God finally unites all created beings to the divine. That is God as Trinity, three 'movements within the dynamic yet stable mystery that we call "Being"' (Macquarrie, 1966, p. 198). Movements are forms of divine action, but they are not just successive ways of acting. They each cooperate in every divine act, necessarily and irreducibly, so that they cannot exist apart or be collapsed into one another.

A movement is not just a blind and directionless alteration. It is a change or action, and as such it entails knowledge, evaluation, intention, and enjoyment. Therefore the Being in which there are three forms of movement, three forms of action, however much it is beyond human comprehension, must be conceived as at least a knowing, intentional, feeling agent, existing in three distinct but necessarily inter-related forms of being and action. Macquarrie names these forms as the primordial (the source of all possibilities), the expressive (expressing or manifesting itself in and through particular beings and 'above all in the finite being of Jesus'), and the unitive (uniting finite beings with Being itself). In every divine act, God is active as the primordial source of possibilities, the creative power that gives form to actual beings, and the unitive power which works to include them in the final goal of Being.

There are echoes here of Whitehead's threefold articulation of God. For Whitehead, God has a primordial aspect, as the conceptual array of all possibilities, though 'deficient in actuality'. In reaction to the process of the world (the everlasting existence of a multiplicity of actual entities, which are the many causes of the creative processes of the world), God has a consequential aspect, including all temporal process in the 'perfected actuality' of the divine consciousness. Finally, God has a superjective aspect, as the contents of the divine consciousness pass back into the temporal world, giving rise to a succession of new initial aims. 'What is done in the world is transformed into a reality in heaven, and floods back again into the world' (Whitehead, 1978, p. 351).

Process philosophy has proved to be too speculative and ambitious for most contemporary philosophers and theologians. But it has provided a set of concepts which can be helpful for thinking about a more definitely Christian idea of God. One obvious difference from most Christian views is that, for Whitehead, there is no 'aboriginal, eminently real, transcendent creator, at whose fiat the world came into being' (Whitehead, 1978, p. 342). Macquarrie, like Whitehead, opposes the model of a monarchical and all-determining divine person. He too wishes to make room for the reality of time, of creativity, and of real creaturely causal power. But unlike Whitehead, he insists on the ultimate causal primacy of God, who expresses the divine being in and through temporal events. And, more consistently with Christian belief, he sees God not only as 'the fellow-sufferer who understands', but also as the one who includes all finite persons in an ultimate communion of love. God is not only primordial and superjective, but God enters into the conditions of finite being in a positive and transformative way, and finally includes finite living persons in the divine being. As Athanasius put it, God became human so that humanity could become divine.

The Trinity as conceived in this way need not be confined to Christian faith, though in Macquarrie and in this book it is based on and suggested by Christian belief. It is about how, in this universe,

Being by its very nature generates beings, expresses itself in and through beings, and unites them to Being, thus fulfilling a goal inherent in the cosmos as a whole. It is about how the cosmos is a goal-directed unity, intended, directed, and fulfilled by a reality beyond or underlying it. That process of conceiving possible beings, actualising them, setting an ideal goal for them, and influencing and enabling them to achieve that goal did not have to be expressed by incarnation, death, and resurrection, or by the founding of a church, a community of the Spirit shaped by an ideal derived from the life of a young human male. Indeed, there exist non-Christian versions of a threefold movement of a supreme Spirit, from conception through expression to liberation and unity. Bradley's Absolute Idealism, by which Macquarrie was influenced in his younger years, is a case in point. Plotinus' neo-Platonism and some versions of Vedantic thought, like that of Ramanuja, are others. They differ significantly from Christianity in many respects, and that is not irrelevant. But there is a general structure of thought here that is not uniquely Christian. There are, as we might expect if God is a God of universal love, vestiges of the Trinity throughout the created world.

The Trinity as we know it can thus be seen as a contingent expression of the divine being. What Macquarrie calls the primordial, expressive, and unitive forms of divine action are co-present and cooperative in every divine act. They could have been expressed in other specific ways, and in other worlds perhaps they are, but they seem to describe the most general characteristics of the divine being as the spiritual source, support, and goal of any and every cosmos we can conceive. I think it is important to see the Trinity in this expanded cosmic form now that we are aware for the first time in history of the vast extent of the universe and the possibility of many forms of life very different from our own in relation to which the same God that we worship must be present if God truly exists as creator of the cosmos.

On this planet, too, there may be diverse forms of revelation as the infinite God is disclosed to and responded to by different peoples with different histories and cultures. The Christian claim is that God reveals the divine nature and purpose through the history of the Jewish people, which for Christians reaches a decisive transformational point with the life, death, and resurrection of Jesus. In him, his followers see an authentic disclosure of the moral ideal for human life in relation to God and the decisive expression of a divine act of self-sacrificial love which can liberate humans from their alienated state of self-absorption. Jesus is 'Son of God' as the one who embodies the eternal Word of God in human form. In relation to him, the Creator is the 'Father', whose role is to nourish, guide, and lead human life to mature freedom and love of the Good. The power of the Spirit which filled Jesus' life continues in the lives of his disciples, uniting them to the divine life as it was expressed in Jesus.

Thus the Trinity is authentically known to human beings as Father, Son, and Spirit. The Father brings into being free value-creating persons. They fall into alienation and spiritual death. Jesus expresses the sacrificial, agapic, love of the Father which liberates them into true freedom. The Spirit is the divine power that empowers them inwardly to prepare them for communion with the divine in a life that transcends bodily death. In this contingent history, the threefold God is known in a specific way – not perhaps the only way, but a way uniquely fitted to enable human beings to find fulfilment in God. If this is so, then our final communion with God will be a participation in a community of personal beings beyond our imagination, with forms of life, knowledge, and action that are limitless. In this life, seeing God as Trinitarian or threefold enables humans to revere a transcendent and indestructible source of supreme value; to imitate Jesus as one who fully expresses the divine character and the human ideal of reconciling and, if occasions demand it, of suffering love; and to progressively achieve participation in the nature of God through the energising and inward power of the divine life. That, for Christians, is an overwhelming reason for living 'in the name of the Father, the Son, and the Holy Spirit' and for seeing this as a fulfilment, and not a denial, of monotheistic belief.

Bibliography

Alston, William, 'Substance and the Trinity', in *The Trinity* (1999)

Aquinas, Thomas, *Summa Contra Gentiles 1*

Aquinas, Thomas, *Summa Theologiae*, vol. 2 (1a.2–11), trans. Timothy McDermott (Blackfriars, 1964)

Ashton, John (ed.), *The Interpretation of John* (SPCK, 1986)

Barth, Karl, *Church Dogmatics 1, The Doctrine of the Word of God*, trans. G. T. Thomson, ch. 2, part 1, 'The Triune God' (T and T Clark, 1936)

Bornkamm, Gunther, 'Towards the Interpretation of John's Gospel', in Ashton (1986)

British Council of Churches, *The Forgotten Trinity* (1989)

Brown, David, *The Divine Trinity* (Duckworth, 1985)

Brown, David, 'Trinitarian Personhood and Individuality', in Feenstra and Plantinga (1989)

Brown, Raymond, *The Community of the Beloved Disciples* (Chapman, 1979)

Clark, Kelly, 'Trinity or Tritheism', *Religious Studies* 32 (1996)

Coakley, Sarah, 'Persons in the Social Doctrine of the Trinity: A Critique of Current Analytic Discussion', in Alston, *The Trinity* (1999)

Coakley, Sarah, 'Why Three? Some Further Reflections of the Doctrine of the Trinity', in S. Coakley and D. A. Pailin (eds.), *The Making and Remaking of Christian Doctrine* (Clarendon, 1993)

Conway Morris, Simon, *Life's Solution* (Cambridge University Press, 2003)

Craig, William, in Craig and Moreland, *Philosophical Foundations for a Christian Worldview* (IVF, 2003)

Craig, William Lane, 'Towards a Tenable Social Trinitarianism', in McCall and Rae (2009)

Cross, Richard, 'Latin Trinitarianism', in McCall and Rae (2009)

Dalferth, Ingolf, 'The Eschatological Roots of the Doctrine of the Trinity', in Schwöbel (1995)

Davis, Stephen, Kendall, Daniel, and O'Collins, Gerald, *The Trinity* (Oxford University Press, 1999)

Dodd, C. H., *The Interpretation of the Fourth Gospel* (Cambridge University Press, 1953)

Feenstra, R. J., and Plantinga, Cornelius, *Trinity, Incarnation and Atonement* (Notre Dame, 1989)

Ford, David, 'What about the Trinity?' in F. Young and D. Ford (eds.), *Meaning and Truth in 2 Corinthians* (Eerdmans, 1987)

Gunton, Colin, *The Promise of Trinitarian Theology* (T and T Clark, 1997)

Haight, Roger, 'The Point of Trinitarian Theology', *Toronto Journal of Theology* 4 (1988)

Harris, Harriet, 'Should We Say That Personhood Is Relational?' *SJT* 51 (1998)

Hasker, William, *Metaphysics and the Tri-Personal God* (Oxford University Press, 2013)

Heschel, Abraham, *The Prophets* (Harper and Row, 1962)

Hill, W. J., *The Three-Personed God* (Catholic University of America, 1982)

Hodgson, Leonard, *The Doctrine of the Trinity* (Nisbet, 1943)

Howard-Snyder, Daniel, 'Trinity Monotheism', in McCall and Rea (2009)

Hughes, Christopher, *On a Complex Theory of a Simple God* (Cornell, 1988)

Hurtado, Larry, *Lord Jesus Christ: Devotion to Jesus in Earliest Christianity* (Eerdmans, 2006)

Hurtado, Larry, 'Summary and Concluding Observations', in Hurtado and Paul Owen (eds.), *Who Is This Son of Man?* (T and T Clark, 2011)

Jenson, Robert, *The Triune Identity* (Fortress, 1982)

Jenson, Robert, 'What Is the Point of Trinitarian Theology?' in Schwöbel (1995)

Jungel, Eberhard, *The Trinity: God's Being Is in Becoming* (Eerdmans, 1976)

Kasemann, Ernst, *Essays on New Testament Themes*, trans. W. J. Montague (SCM Press, 1964)

Kasper, Walter, *The God of Jesus Christ* (Crossroad, 1984)

Kretzmann, Norman, in Scott MacDonald (ed.), *Being and Goodness* (Cornell University Press, 1991)

Kretzmann, Norman, *The Metaphysics of Theism: Aquinas' Natural Theology in Summa Contra Gentiles 1* (Clarendon, 1997)

Lacugna, Catherine, *God for Us* (Harper, 1991)

Layman, Stephen, 'Tritheism and the Trinity', *Faith and Philosophy* 5 (1988)

Leftow, Brian, 'Anti-Social Trinitarianism', in McCall and Rae (2009)

Leftow, Brian, 'A Latin Trinity', *Faith and Philosophy* 21/3 (July, 2004)

Leftow, Brian, 'Modes without Persons', in van Inwagen and Zimmerman (eds.), *Persons Human and Divine* (Clarendon, 2007)

Leftow, Brian, 'Time-Travel and the Trinity', in *Faith and Philosophy* 29/3 (July, 2012)

Leslie, John, *Infinite Minds* (Clarendon, 2001)

Lindars, Barnabas, *John* (JSOT Press, University of Sheffield, 1990)

Mackey, John, *The Christian Experience of God as Trinity* (SCM Press, 1983)

Macquarrie, John, *Principles of Christian Theology* (SCM Press, 1966)

McCall, Thomas, *Which Trinity? Whose Monotheism?* (Eerdmans, 2010)

McCall, Thomas, and Rae, Michael, *Philosophical and Theological Essays on the Trinity* (Oxford University Press, 2009)

Meeks, Wayne, 'The Man from Heaven in Johannine Sectarianism', in Ashton (ed.) *The Interpretation of John* (SPCK, 1986)

Moltmann, Jurgen, *The Trinity and the Kingdom of God*, trans. M. Kohl (SCM Press, 1981)

Morris, Thomas, *The Logic of God Incarnate* (Cornell University Press, 1986)

Mosser, Carl, 'Fully Social Trinitarianism', in McCall and Rea (2009)

Pannenberg, Wolfhart, *Systematic Theology*, vol. 1 (T and T Clark, 1992), ch. 5, 'The Trinitarian God', and ch. 6, para. 7a, 'Love and Trinity'

Peters, Ted, *God as Trinity* (Westminster, 1993)

Phan, Peter, *The Cambridge Companion to the Trinity* (Cambridge University Press, 2011)

Plantinga, Cornelius, 'The Social Analogy of the Trinity', *The Thomist* 50 (1986)

Rae, Michael, 'The Trinity', in Rae and Flint (eds.), *Oxford Handbook of Philosophical Theology* (Oxford University Press, 2009)

Rahner, Karl, *Theological Investigations, 4: Remarks on the Dogmatic Treatise 'De Trinitate'*, trans. K. Smith (Darton, Longman & Todd, 1966)

Rahner, Karl, 'The Trinity', trans. J. Donceel (Burns and Oates, 1979)

Richard of St. Victor, *De Trinitate*, 3

Schoonenberg, 'Trinity: The Consummated Covenant', *Studies in Religion* 5 (1975)

Schwöbel, Christoph, *Trinitarian Theology Today* (T and T Clark, 1995)

Stead, G. C., *Divine Substance* (Clarendon, 1977)

Swinburne, Richard, *The Christian God* (Oxford University Press, 1994)

Swinburne, Richard, *The Coherence of Theism* (Oxford University Press, 1977)

Swinburne, Richard, 'Could There Be More Than One God?' *Faith and Philosophy* 5 (1988)

Thompson, John, *Modern Trinitarian Perspectives* (Oxford University Press, 1994)

Torrance, Alan, *Persons in Communion* (T and T Clark, 1996)

Van Inwagen, Peter, 'And Yet There Are Not Three Gods, but One God', in T. V. Morris (ed.), *Philosophy and the Christian Faith* (Notre Dame, 1988)

Von Balthasar, Hans Urs, *Theo-Drama; Theological Dramatic Theory* 4 (San Francisco: Ignatius Press, 1994)

Ward, Keith, *Morality, Autonomy, and God* (Oneworld Publications, 2013)

Ward, Keith, *Religion and Creation* (Clarendon, 1996)

Welch, Claude, *In This Name* (Scribners, 1952)

Welch, Claude, *The Trinity in Contemporary Theology* (SCM Press, 1953)

Whitehead, A. N., *Process and Reality* [1929] corrected ed. D. R. Griffin and D. W. Sherburne (eds.) (Macmillan, 1978)

Wierenga, Edward, 'Trinity and Polytheism', *Faith and Philosophy* 21/3 (July, 2004), p. 287

Wiggins, David, *Sameness and Substance* (Blackwell, 1980)

Wiles, Maurice, 'Some Reflections on the Origins of the Doctrine of the Trinity', *JTS* 8 (1957)

Wiles, Maurice, 'Why Three?' in *The Making of Christian Doctrine* (Cambridge University Press, 1967)

Williams, C. J. F., 'Neither Confounding the Persons nor Dividing the Substance', in Alan Padgett (ed.), *Reason and the Christian Religion* (Oxford University Press, 1994)

Williams, Rowan, 'Trinity and Ontology', in K. Surin (ed.) *Christ, Ethics, and Tragedy* (Cambridge University Press, 1989)

Williams, Rowan, 'Trinity and Revelation', *Modern Theology* 2 (1986)

Yandell, Keith, 'How Many Times Does Three Go into One?', in MacCall and Rae (2009)

Yandell, Keith, 'Trinity and Consistency', *Religious Studies* 30 (1994)

Zizioulas, John, 'The Doctrine of the Trinity: The Cappadocian Contribution', in Schwöbel (ed.), *Trinitarian Theology Today* (1995)

Zizioulas, John, 'Personhood and Being', in *Being as Communion* (DLT, 1985)

Subject Index

Name Index

Lightning Source UK Ltd.
Milton Keynes UK
UKHW02f0850070318
319030UK00010B/77/P